A Guide to

TIBET

Elisabeth B. Booz

COLLINS

8 Grafton Street, London W1

William Collins Sons and Co. Ltd
London. Glasgow. Sydney. Auckland
Toronto. Johannesburg

British Library Cataloguing in Publication Data

Booz, Elisabeth B.
A guide to Tibet.
1. Tibet (China) Description and travel
Guide books
I. Title
915.1'50458   DS786

ISBN 0-00-217627-0

First published 1986
© Shangri-La Press

From The Trekker's Guide to the Himalaya and Karakoram by Hugh Swift. Tibetan Glossary by
Milan M. Melvin. Copyright © 1982 by Hugh Swift.
Reprinted by permission of Sierra Club Books.

Photographs by Jacky Yip (4-5, 23, 27, 30, 52-53, 60-61, 72-73, 88-89, 93, 99, 107,
146-147, 154, 158-159); China Guides Series (7, 13, 16, 19, 49, 56-57, 64-65, 76-77,
80-81, 84-85, 108-109, 111, 116, 141, 168, 176); Stone Routes (97, 103, 132-133, 136-137,
144, 164-165); Herman Wong (69, 104-105, 172-173); Kate Kranzler (129); Tom Laird (161)

Maps, diagrams and artwork: Li Design Associates

Printed in Hong Kong

Contents

Maps

Introduction

by David Bonavia

Even for the most seasoned traveller, the first sight of Tibet from the air is a riveting experience.

The daily flight from Chengdu, in China's westernmost province of Sichuan, reaches Lhasa over spectacular, forbidding mountain ranges — banking steeply to swoop down into a delicately green valley under the intense deep blue of the Tibetan sky.

The first impression is one of absolute silence, as passengers file out of the aircraft and cautiously sniff the rarified air, two miles above sea-level.

Lhasa is two hours' drive from the airstrip, and the journey is spectacular. A broad, swift river runs by the road for much of the way, fed by the melting snows of the mountains that stand around in craggy ranks.

Geological developments constantly change the land, almost in front of one's eyes. Fierce winds, rain and ice attack the rock and tumble it year by year into ever-new screes and landslips, fine sand and rolling boulders. A flush of dark green here and there betrays the presence of scraggy grass or moss. By the roadside, a few dried-up shrubs struggle for survival.

How can human beings survive in such country? On the road to Lhasa, only a few tiny hamlets of stone and mud-brick are to be seen, with a handful of women in long black skirts chasing goats or milling barley with a flat stone.

The river brings life and beauty to the land for short stretches on either side of its course. Cattle browse in the fresh grass; here and there someone has planted a tiny crop of vegetables or tobacco; even a few small trees have found sustenance for their roots. But over it all tower the mountains, rolling in immense ranges on all sides, with only a few valleys where permanent habitation is possible.

Tibet — with a population of about 1.8 million and an area of nearly half a million square miles — is one of the most sparsely inhabited places anywhere in the world. Lying mostly above 4,500 m. (15,000 ft.), its height above sea-level is to be compared only with Bolivia's.

The land can support only the most robust crops — especially hill-barley, which is the the staple food of the people. Yaks, cows, horses, sheep and goats provide protein in the form of milk, cheese and meat, and the prevalent smell everywhere — even on the traveller's clothes after leaving Tibet — is that of yak butter mingled with the smoke of fires of dried dung.

Much of the rugged terrain is impassable in winter, when temperatures can fall as low as −40°C (−40°F) with cutting winds and heavy snowfalls. There are few motorable roads and no railways. However, modern roads nowadays connect Lhasa with the provinces of Sichuan and Qinghai, and there are regular scheduled flights from Chengdu and from Golmud, in Qinghai. Tibet's border with Nepal opened recently, in 1985, but the other extensive borders with India, Burma, Sikkim and Bhutan are still mostly closed to outsiders.

Lhasa, the capital of Tibet, is believed to have been founded some 14 centuries ago around the time when Buddhism was introduced during the reign of the celebrated King Songtsen Gampo. Nowadays, it is really two cities — the modern Chinese part with straight, tree-lined streets and relatively modern architecture; and the old Tibetan city, where rain can turn crooked streets into seas of mud.

The architecture of the Tibetan city takes the form of solid stone buildings, some three storeys high, with elaborately carved wooden eaves.In this part of Lhasa one can share the daily life of the Tibetan people, as they offer their wares at the curbside, chant prayers to themselves while seated cross-legged on the ground, or burn juniper bushes to please gods with the aroma.

The market is lively with stalls selling fresh mutton, brightly coloured knitting wool, pots, kettles and the handsome, nearly four-foot high, brass churns in which Tibetans like to brew their tea mixed with yak butter. Huge lumps of the rich yellow yak butter are brought to the market in skins.There are also trinkets and personal ornaments, rosaries, tinder-purses and knives for sale.

Charms and amulets not only signify a person's respect for the spirit world, but are also considered to have specific magical powers to ward off disease, accidents and misfortunes, bullets, dog-bites, attacks by eagles, and so forth.

The rosaries are supposed to contain 108 beads of uniform size, and are held in the right hand when they are being counted. When they are not in use they are wound round the left wrist like a bracelet or worn around the neck. They may contain beads of wood, seeds, bone, glass, crystal, turquoise or ivory.

The people of Tibet — believed on the evidence of their language to be remotely related to the Chinese and the Burmese — are of uncertain origin. Their recorded history does not extend back further than the 7th century, when for the first time they acquired a writing system along with the newly imported religion of Buddhism.

Of varying build in different parts of the country, the Tibetans have the high cheekbones and sallow complexion of the Mongoloids, and they pursue a lifestyle similar to that of the Mongolian and Turkic peoples of Central Asia. Agriculture, stockbreeding and herding are the mainstays of life. Since ancient times their society was dominated by a feudal aristocracy living off the labour of a mass of bondsmen. With the advent of Buddhism, huge monasteries sprang up which also lived off the produce of the herdsmen and farmers, and took nearly one fifth of the country's males out of productive work.

The Tibetans have been called the most religious people in the world. Religion in traditional Tibetan life is not a matter of occasional ritual observances and acceptance of a particular code of belief and behaviour. For all their recorded history, religion has been an integral part of the Tibetans' everyday life. Women walk down the street twirling a small prayer wheel, confident that with every turn they accumulate merit in this life and will obtain a better reincarnation in the next. Aromatic shrubs — usually juniper — are burned in public places, as much for their value as offerings as their spiritual significance, for the smoke from their fires is believed to carry prayers to the gods and be a defence against evil spirits. People bring thermos flasks of hot yak butter to add to the reservoirs of the lamps in monasteries and other holy places.

When obliged to commit an act which, strictly speaking, is contrary to Buddhism — such as slaughtering an animal for food — a Tibetan will simultaneously offer up a prayer for forgiveness. Religion is seen as helping people to communicate on a higher plane with each other and with the spirit world, and as counteracting such human tendencies as cupidity, malice, or vengefulness.

Many of the special features of Tibetan Buddhism derive from the fact that it superseded, and in some ways absorbed, the ancient Tibetan religion called Bon. This is a primitive kind of animism in which rocks, trees, rivers and mountain passes are thought to be the homes of spirits who must be placated with small offerings whenever one passes them. And like other proto-religious creeds — in Siberia, in Africa, or among the Australian Aboriginals or American Indians — Bon has shamans, or priestly adepts, who can go into trances to cure sickness, exorcise demons, or communicate with spirits and the dead.

There are no authenticated texts of the early Bon religion, since writing was introduced to Tibet at roughly the same time as Buddhism, which sought to supplant the barbaric old creed with its superstitious beliefs and practices. Though Buddhism has had the upper hand for most of Tibet's religious history, the more broad-minded of the lamas have accepted Bon as a kindred religion whose aims are to some extent the same as those of Buddhism — banishing suffering and increasing people's spiritual awareness. In some parts of Tibet, Bon is still practised; but the making of offerings at shrines and places believed to harbour spirits has been subsumed into Buddhism, and the many-coloured strips of cloth or "prayer flags", which probably owe their origins to Bon, are nowadays seen as tokens of a strong Buddhist faith.

Tibetan Buddhists cling to the idea of the efficacy of prayer — the more the better. The prayer wheel, which can be small enough to hold in the hand, or as big as a man, is seen everywhere. Small printed prayers and invocations are sold by the million.

Ceremonial silk scarves — *kata* — are exchanged on many occasions as a courtesy ritual. Sometimes they, too, are hung up with prayer flags, or draped on a holy image.

Numerous travellers have remarked on the amiability of the Tibetan people, and their love of life and fellowship. They revere nature, and respect and cherish animals even when they must kill them for food. Their lifestyle is aimed at achieving a harmonious balance between their daily chores and the spiritual forces which they believe to exist all around them.

The Tibetans are naturally likeable people, but they are as prone to human weakness as anyone. Throughout their history, bandits, oppressive rulers and profligates, often sheltering behind the badge of the monk or lama, have clashed with the high ideals and abstruse philosophy of Buddhism. Generally, however, the Tibetans show attractive characteristics, offering open and direct friendliness to strangers and to each other, and preserving a sense of humour. They have a strong belief in the spiritual nature of man, while recognising the inevitability of human foibles. Their intimate contact with soil, mountain, beast and bird also bestows on them an air of spontaneity and inner freedom.

Hardly ever will a foreigner encounter a scowl from Lhasa's Tibetan population. Extreme curiosity and immense goodness shine in the expressions of the weather-beaten faces. The Tibetans like to be photographed, though sometimes they are a little disappointed at not getting an immediate print. The Polaroid camera is one solution, but often all the pictures will be snapped up by the people in the crowd, leaving none for the photographer.

Information on the Tibetan people before the 7th century is vague, wreathed in innumerable legends about the origins of the world with Tibet at its centre. Some Tibetans believe the world was created from a lump of butter which congealed out of a sea of milk.

In their isolation and rugged territory, the Tibetans of ancient times lived in independent kingdoms, waging fierce war on their neighbours, the Chinese, Mongols and others, harassing the outposts of the Chinese Empire, and plundering whenever they had the opportunity.

Early in China's Tang Dynasty (7th to 10th centuries AD), more civilised forms of contacts between the two countries were adopted. Tibet's most famous king, Songtsen Gampo, married a Chinese princess, Wen Cheng, who helped introduce Buddhism, as did his other foreign wife, a Nepalese. Despite recurrent periods of conflict, Tibet absorbed much of Chinese culture and civilisation, and its people became accustomed to the use of silks, book-learning, and, above all, tea-drinking.

With the consolidation of Buddhism as the dominant spiritual force in Tibet, the rulers cultivated complex and shifting relationships with their other powerful neighbours, the Mongols. The Mongol Kublai Khan subjugated China in the 13th century, and Tibetan Buddhism became the official creed at the court of later Mongol rulers.

In the 17th century, towards the end of the Chinese Ming Dynasty which had overthrown Mongolian rule three centuries earlier, one branch of the Mongol race invaded Tibet and occupied Lhasa. To forestall further loss of influence in Tibet, the Qing (Ch'ing) emperor, who overthrew the Ming in 1644, sent an expeditionary force to recapture Lhasa and impose Chinese suzerainty over the whole country. But Tibet's indigenous culture had by now matured to the point where little more was absorbed from China: indeed, the spiritual ruler, the Dalai Lama, exercised some influence in Peking, where the Buddhist-inclined Qing emperors maintained facilities for Lamaism, to which they inclined even after the reconfirmation of Confucianism as the state creed for China.

The Chinese presence in Lhasa, never very big until recent times, was enlarged to meet the threat of encroachment from British-ruled India and Tsarist Russia in the 19th century. A British expeditionary force reached Lhasa in 1904, imposed a treaty and then withdrew. Two years later, it was agreed between Britain and China that neither should rule Tibet, but China soon re-established her loose suzerainty, despite recurring rebellions and internal power struggles.

Tibet's isolation from all but a few intrepid travellers continued until 1951, when the victorious People's Liberation Army of the Chinese Communists reached Lhasa after conquering the Kuomintang (Nationalist) forces led by Chiang Kai-shek. For nearly a decade, the Chinese interfered little in the traditional way of life, but it was not in their nature to delay forever the modernisation of Tibet. In 1959, following increased friction with the Chinese occupation forces and a growing armed rebellion, the Dalai Lama fled to India, where he resides to this day.

Tibet was then to all intents and purposes under military-backed Chinese rule, and the protection of its frontiers and strengthening of the armed Chinese presence there took priority. The Chinese also set about disbanding the several thousand monasteries, enjoining monks, nuns and lamas to take productive jobs and cease their "parasitic" existence.

After the closure of the monasteries, an extensive propaganda campaign was organised to expose what were claimed to be cruel atrocities practised by the monasteries and the feudal gentry class to keep the serfs in bondage and submission.

It is hard to know what to make of these charges. Western travellers in Tibet, right up to the time of the Chinese occupation, seem to have witnessed little of such cruelty, though doubtless such incidents occurred; mutilation, for instance, was a standard punishment, as in the Islamic world. Officials in Lhasa will nowadays admit that the stories of atrocities may have been exaggerated — while insisting on their basic veracity.

The Chinese built new roads and airfields, so that Tibet was brought to within a few hours' journey from the Chinese heartland. Marxism was introduced in the school curriculum — more notionally than actually, for the

country is still desperately short of qualified teachers. Previously, all education had been in the hands of monks and lamas, who taught mostly Tibetan script, Buddhist scripture and Tibetan myths and legends, together with rhetoric, logic and esoteric studies for advanced pupils. The lamas were not — as often alleged — entirely parasitic, for they preserved Tibet's fine artistic and architectural traditions and voluminous literature, collected medical knowledge and practised herbal cures.

Throughout the 1950s and early '60s, vague reports of armed resistance by the Tibetans reached the outside world. Foreign opinion on Tibet tended to be polarised between those who thought the Chinese were performing a civilising mission, as was their historic duty, and those who saw the Chinese presence in Tibet as the murder of Tibetan culture and the killing or imprisonment of all those who resisted.

The question of China's sovereignty over Tibet has long been a subject of controversy — a controversy which nowadays is mainly academic, since there is *no* question of China renouncing her rule of the huge region.

The Chinese see their role in Tibet as twofold — strategic and social. Firstly, they intend to maintain firm control over a region which, in the past, has attracted the interest of other great powers and which, in the absence of Chinese troops, might fall under the domination of India or the Soviet Union. Secondly, China aims to modernise Tibet and lead its people to socialism. China gains few economic advantages from her position in Tibet — indeed, it is a big drain on investment funds from Peking and produces little of value (except rugs, for which there is an export market). There is the likelihood, however, of useful minerals being extracted in large quantities now that a full geological survey of the country has been made.

In 1980, the Chinese Communist Party dismissed the 1st Party Secretary of Tibet, and announced a series of reforms aimed at assuaging long-standing grievances among the Tibetan people. One of the most important reforms was the granting of nearly full economic autonomy to the Tibetans. Previously, Chinese officials had tried to make more and more people grow winter wheat instead of barley. But apart from the fact that nearly all Tibetans prefer barley to wheat, the soil and weather conditions proved unsuitable for wheat. However, the Chinese did encourage the Tibetans to grow vegetables — which accounted for the rumour spread among Tibetans that the Chinese ate grass.

Farmers, who are now free to grow barley again, are not at present obliged to deliver specific amounts of grain and other produce to the State in order to feed the city-dwellers. They can freely negotiate contracts with purchasing agencies or sell their produce on the open market.

Communication is quite a problem. Few people in Tibet speak Chinese, let alone other languages. Sometimes the hawkers in Lhasa have to enlist the help of a small boy who has learnt a little Chinese in primary school, and who can at least translate prices. The Tibetan language is rich and complex, with an extraordinary system of spelling — including numerous unpronounced letters — which makes even English orthography look simple. Most people over 40 appear to be illiterate, even in Tibetan.

Relatively few of the many Chinese technicians and officials — perhaps about 10% — speak even passable Tibetan, either. Many of them would rather return to China proper than stay in this austere land with its alien culture, paucity of oxygen to breathe and lack of fresh food to eat. But the State pays extra cash allowances for service in Tibet, so people posted there can send a more generous allowance to their families back home in the plains. Chinese officials are now being gradually withdrawn to speed the promotion of their Tibetan counterparts.

The most urgent priority is to increase the number of school teachers, fluent in both Tibetan and Chinese, in order to bridge the huge cultural gap still existing between the two cultures. The authorities have already promised that greater respect and attention will be shown in future to the teaching of the Tibetan written language and the study of Tibetan culture and literature. How far these promised reforms will be implemented in practice, only time will tell.

A more liberal attitude is also being taken by the Chinese in the 1980s towards the Buddhist religion, in accordance with a nationwide policy of ending the suppression by the Party and State of organised religion in all forms. Some of Tibet's more famous old monasteries are being restored and re-opened to the public. The number of them at which religious observances are held has increased, and the throng of people, young and old, who attend with every show of piety, indicates that the official effort to spread the ideas of Marxist atheism has had little effect.

The people have responded to the new, more tolerant atmosphere with a wave of enthusiasm for their religion — Buddhism of the Mahayana or "Greater Vehicle" school, blended with Tantric practices partly imported from India, and elements of the old animist or spirit-worshipping religion, Bon.

It is unlikely that young men will again be permitted to enter the monasteries in significant numbers, but the present Chinese policy appears to be to let a few take up the religious life, if only to encourage a semblance of religious freedom and keep track of the faithful devotees by allowing them more open means of worship.

Particularly controversial in the 1980s is the question of the possible return of the Dalai Lama to Tibet. Chinese officials in Peking and Lhasa seem divided in their opinion as to whether and under what conditions the Dalai Lama should be permitted to return. Some evidently feel that his presence would be too disruptive because so many Tibetans still think of him as a "living Buddha" — the reincarnation of Chenrezi, Lord of Mercy, and the God-King of Tibet. Others — though in recent years these have become far

fewer — think he could be given an honorary position in the government and be permitted to act as the spiritual head of Tibetan believers.

The problem hinges on whether the Chinese believe that Buddhism in Tibet is dying a natural death, or whether they see it as a still powerful force opposing their attempts at modernisation of Tibetan society. At the Jokhang Temple in central Lhasa, for example, believers flock to worship on each of the six days a week when it is open for this purpose. They include many young people dressed in Chinese-style tunic and trousers but obviously still clinging to the religion of their ancestors. Many prostrate themselves full-length on the threshold. Inside, people push and squeeze to file through the tiny shrines where relics and votive objects are kept and monks distribute blessings and say prayers.

To visit any Tibetan temple or monastery is an eerie, and to some people disturbing, experience. In the yellow half-light of dozens of strong-smelling yak butter lamps, and the pale wreaths of incense, one gazes up at the inhumanly calm or fierce expressions of Bodhisattvas, gods and demons, sculpted in huge effigies. Some are clothed in immense robes of brocade and gold thread. On shelves behind them lie stacks of dusty scriptures.

Less foreboding a sight in these temples is the deity embraced by a woman — symbolising the union of wisdom and compassion. In one hand he holds a small bell, and in the other a bronze thunderbolt, symbol of spiritual power. Below the images, coins lie scattered around — offerings from pilgrims. Many walls are covered from top to bottom in magnificent, detailed mural paintings, depicting temples and gardens, demons and gods, heavens and hells, monks, lamas and ordinary people going about their daily affairs.

The reality of everyday life is, of course, rather less ornate, though conditions for ordinary people are improving in some areas, particularly in Lhasa where there has been a recent attempt to improve hygiene and sanitation. Better communications by road and air have also brought in new foodstuffs to Lhasa though a big effort has been put into making Lhasa at least self-sufficient in vegetables such as onions, chillies, tomatoes and beans. Such hardy fruits as pears and apples are also grown.

One item, however, has been imported to Tibet for centuries and has become an essential ingredient in the Tibetans' daily life: tea, the main drink in Tibet, is also an important form of nutrition, for it is taken together with yak butter and often barley meal (tsampa) as well. Dozens of cups of tea may be drunk in a single day. The tea itself comes from China proper, in the shape of hard, compressed bricks. While it is infusing, a little wood-ash soda may be added to improve the colour. The infused tea is then strained into a copper or brass churn, where it is thoroughly mixed with some yak butter. The final beverage — more like a soup than tea — is put in kettles ready for drinking. Most people carry wooden bowls (some of them with silver decorations and lids) into which they pour their tea. The drink is also used to moisten barley flour, which can then be rolled into a pellet and eaten.

The other national beverage is *chang*, a barley beer of a pale grey colour, faintly effervescent and slightly sour. A more potent spirit (arak) can be distilled from the beer. On the whole, the farmers and traders drink more alcohol then the nomadic herdsmen.

Visitors are sometimes embarrassed by the assiduity with which Tibetan hosts insist on refilling their cups or bowls. This is simply a local custom and sign of courtesy; the visitor who does not wish to drink more can flick a little of the liquid in the air or drink a whole cup or bowl and decline a refill.

Tibetan people are divided into two main categories — those who remain in one place, cultivating the land and conducting commerce, and those who still cling to the nomadic life, driving their herds of yak and other cattle to fresh pastures — the higher ones in summer, the lower ones in the severe winter.

The nomads live in felt tents, made from yak hair moistened, beaten and squeezed time and time again until it sticks together in a thick, cold-resistant layer. The tents, stretched over a framework and made secure with lines and pegs, are warm and comfortable. But the young people, especially the men, like to sleep in the open air under the stars, sometimes snuggling up to sheep for warmth. Even in sub-zero temperatures, they consider this the healthiest way to sleep and rarely suffer frostbite.

They eat mostly cheese, meat and *tsampa*. Although there is some wildlife, the nomads prefer to slaughter their own domestic animals, and regard the beasts of the wild as dangerous enemies, to be guarded against with primitive firearms, slingshots and fierce dogs.

They travel in groups of families, sometimes totalling scores or even hundreds of people, consulting carefully among themselves as to the best pastures to move to. Sometimes they visit the towns or settlements of the farmers camping in the outskirts and conducting a little desultory barter-trade.

Bandits used to be numerous in the hills and passes of the more remote regions, and their depredations were accepted as a fact of everyday life for groups of people on the move without adequate protection. The introduction of motor vehicles, helicopters and radio communications has probably reduced their activities to a near-negligible level. Following China's assumption of military control in Tibet, many of the bandits — especially the Khampa tribesmen from eastern Tibet — carried on guerrilla warfare against the Chinese army. But in a land with so little forest cover and so few means of sustenance, it would not be difficult for the security forces to harass them, kill or capture their fighting men, or starve them out through surveillance of their base areas. In recent years there have been no substantiated reports of insurgent activity.

Among the favourite weapons of the Tibetan nomad is the rifle or musket, with antelope horns (or substitutes for them) branching out from the sides of the muzzle, to provide a stable rest for sharpshooting. This attachment can be folded under the barrel when not required. The throwing spear has a coil of cord attached so that the thrower can recover it if it misses its mark. Knives come in all shapes and sizes. The slingshot is made of yak hair and can launch a small stone — with deadly effect — from impressive distances.

Sports include target practice from horseback — with rifle or spear — as well as horse-racing and wrestling.

The men nearly all carry sharp knives under their folded *chuba* — a multi-folded coat, often thrown off one shoulder and serving as a kind of voluminous pouch in which the wearer's personal effects are carried. The knives are sometimes very large and sharp and often encased in exquisitely wrought silver-and-wood sheaths. They are used to slaughter cattle, cut meat and, if necessary, in self-defence.

In terms of dress, the men show considerably more individualism and variety than the women. Standard to all — except the lamas — are the woollen breeches thrust into knee-length boots of felt and yak hide. The upper part of the body is clad in a jerkin and over this, the *chuba* is worn.

Many types of hat are worn — from the traditional fur-and-brocade headpiece shaped like an upside-down flowerpot with ear-flaps, to western-style trilbies and homburgs, which make the men look very much like the Indians of the Andes.

Tibetan women, by contrast, tend to dress alike, with a floor-length black gown, a bodice and a long apron hanging from the waist in stripes of brilliant colours. For headwear, the standard model is a small, pillbox-shaped cap, brocaded, and with a wing-like strip of material protruding at one side.

Certain personal ornaments and religious objects are worn by most of the women. Apart from the prayer wheel carried and rotated as often as possible in the hand, there are silver amulets stuffed with prayers, beads of coral and turquoise (the most commonly found semi-precious stones, mostly of poor quality), S-shaped earrings coiled around the ear with dangling stones or enamel work, a rosary for counting one's prayers, and bracelets of silver or silver alloy. Small statuettes of a *rinpoche* (a title of respect for a venerated lama) are often carried by Tibetan men.

The men and women alike part readily with their personal ornaments for cash, although there has been an attempt by the authorities to ban this practice. The articles Tibetan women are least willing to trade are their prayer wheels and rosaries.

For all the exotic characteristics of Tibetan culture, it has one simple, fundamental goal: to seek man's proper adjustment to the natural world. If the people of Tibet hold fast to this orientation, no amount of modernisation will in the long run be in conflict with their nature and their purposes.

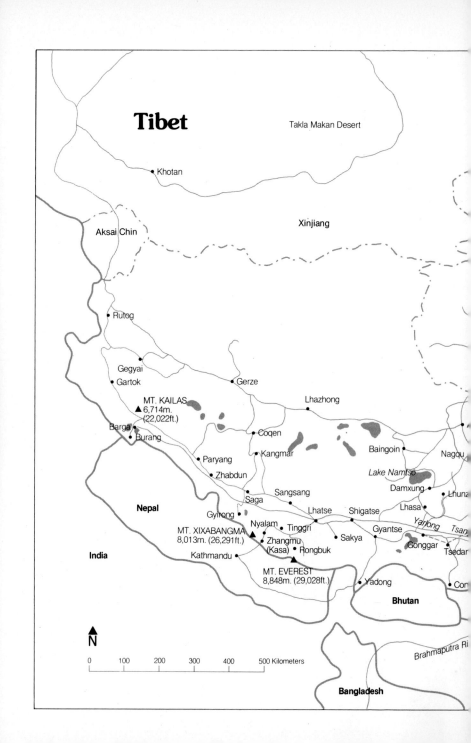

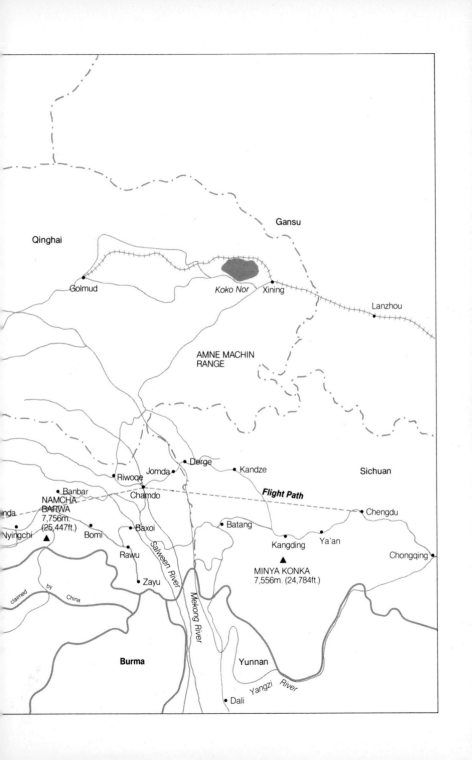

Visiting Tibet

To visit Tibet, the legendary, forbidden land on the roof of the world, has been the lifelong dream of many Westerners. In the past, the dream was also to be among the first to get there, to see Tibet still intact, unspoiled by other tourists. But today, such hopes are unrealistic. Twenty years as a region within the People's Republic of China have brought inevitable changes to Tibet and the rapid development of tourism is tearing holes in its enticing aura of mystery.

Nevertheless, Tibet remains one of the most interesting, remote, undeveloped parts of the world. Its limited facilities for tourists are only now approaching a reasonable standard. Travel outside Lhasa is expensive and difficult. A trip to Tibet is not for everybody — not for the weak, the comfort-loving or the squeamish traveller!

This book does not intend to cover all of Tibet. Bold individuals travelling by bicycle or hitch-hiking on trucks have penetrated nearly every corner of Tibet but this book is concerned mainly with those parts of southern and central Tibet that have been declared open to foreigners by the Chinese. Its aim is to help travellers who want to explore them in depth and understand what they see.

All trips begin in Lhasa, the capital. Lhasa is the centre of administration and authority — for permission to visit other places, for arranging transportation, for buying supplies. Many of Tibet's greatest cultural monuments are concentrated in Lhasa and its altitude below 4,000 m. (12,000 ft.), makes it a good place to begin the trip, to rest, sightsee and become acclimatised.

Getting There

By Air The commonest, quickest way for travellers to reach Lhasa is by air from Chengdu, capital of Sichuan Province. Until early 1985 this was the only entry route permitted for foreigners. Now other options are open.

Chengdu — Gonggar Every day China's airline CAAC (Civil Aviation Administration of China) operates an early morning, two-hour flight by Boeing 707 from Chengdu to Gonggar, the site of Lhasa's airport. Twice a week a second early morning flight by Ilyushin 18 takes 2 hours 50 minutes. Unless travelling with a group under the care of China International Travel Service (CITS, p.35) it is only possible to make a one-way reservation from Chengdu. (Economy US$ 113, First Class US$ 148.) Return reservations can be made at the CAAC office in Lhasa on arrival.

In clear weather the flight from Chengdu offers a spectacular panorama of mountain ranges where many peaks reach 6,700 m. (22,000 ft.). The best view is from the left side of the plane. The many-crested Minya Konka massif

with its 7,556 m. (24,783 ft.) peak stands out dramatically after 20 minutes of flight. Half an hour later the southern horizon reveals 7,756 m. (25,447 ft.) Namcha Barwa, the impenetrable, snow-capped peak that forces Tibet's east-flowing Yarlong Tsangpo River to turn south, then west — to enter India as the Brahmaputra River. Between craggy ranges are glimpses of silver, pencil-line rivers at the bottom of precipitous gorges where some of the Earth's deepest river trenches — the Yangzi, the Mekong, the Salween — run within 50 miles of one another.

Golmud — Gonggar CAAC operates a twice-weekly Ilyushin 18 flight from Golmud, in Qinghai Province, to Gonggar. (US$ 81 one way, single class.) The flight takes 2 hours 10 minutes. Golmud can be reached by air in 2 hours 45 minutes from Xian where the flight originates, or by train in 21 hours from Xining, capital of Qinghai Province.

Kathmandu — Gonggar Talks have been initiated between the governments of China and Nepal regarding international flights to Lhasa via Kathmandu. Chances look good that this route will open soon.

Gonggar — Lhasa Having landed at Gonggar in the Yarlong Tsangpo Valley 90 km. (56 miles) from Lhasa, passengers proceed by CAAC bus or CITS vehicle for a drive of 1½ hours. There is no recognisable airport at Gonggar. Planes discharge passengers and freight at an airstrip, pick up a new load and take off again immediately.

Luggage does not accompany passengers from the airstrip to Lhasa but arrives by truck several hours later. Groups travelling under CITS receive it at their hotel. Others pick it up themselves at the CAAC office (Map, p. 36-37, Useful Addresses, p. 202). In either case it is advisable to bring a small overnight bag as hand luggage on the plane in case the checked luggage gets delayed.

The paved road from Gonggar follows the south bank of the Yarlong Tsangpo River for 25 km. (15½ miles) then crosses a bridge and follows the Kyichu (Quxu) River north for 55 km. (34 miles). At the junction of the Lhasa and Damxung Rivers the valley divides and the golden roofs of Lhasa's Potala Palace can be seen in the distance to the east.

By Road For hardy, adventurous travellers the idea of either entering or leaving Tibet by road holds great appeal, by following in the footsteps of explorers who tried for more than a century to reach Lhasa overland — and usually failed (p.46).

Kathmandu — Lhasa The road route from Nepal to Lhasa is at present restricted to groups booked through tour operators in Kathmandu and registered with CITS. However, all travellers are permitted to exit from Tibet into Nepal. This route is discussed in detail on pp.157-175.

The trip from Nepal to Lhasa usually takes at least three days with overnight stops in Zhangmu (also called Kasa) and Shigatse. Transportation by minibus is arranged by CITS at a cost of Rmb.2.50 per kilometre, though this can occasionally be negotiated downward. The distance from Zhangmu to Lhasa is about 900 km. (560 miles) mostly on unpaved roads. It is a strenuous journey, especially for people who are not yet fully acclimatised to high altitudes. Within the first 90 km. (55 miles) from Zhangmu the road ascends almost 3,000 m. (almost 10,000 ft.) to the Lalung Leh Pass (5,124 m. or 16,806 ft.). Less than 210 km. (130 miles) further it crosses the Jia Tsuo La Pass at 5,252 m. (17,226 ft.). It is a pleasanter, less exhausting trip when taken in the opposite direction after a period of travel and acclimatisation in the region of Lhasa (3,607 m. or 11,830 ft.).

Golmud — Lhasa Tibet's main northern road links Lhasa with Golmud, Qinghai Province, where the railroad terminates. The distance from Golmud to Lhasa is 1,155 km. (720 miles). This is not an officially permitted way to enter Tibet but so many intrepid individuals have used it that it deserves mention. A 48-hour transit permit to visit Golmud can be obtained from any Public Security Bureau and the Golmud Hotel offers simple accommodation to foreigners. Buses and trucks depart for Lhasa on an irregular schedule and may take anywhere from 35 hours (as advertised) to 56 hours. Short stops are made at Amdo, Nagqu and Damxung. Breakdowns are frequent. Passengers bring their own food and protection against cold, as snowstorms can occur on high passes at any time of year. Bus fare is Rmb. 60. Truck fare is negotiable.

Chengdu — Lhasa Tibet's main eastern road crosses precipitous mountain ranges and river gorges from Chengdu by way of Kangding, Derge and Chamdo. It is not officially open to travel for foreigners. The distance from Chengdu to Lhasa is approximately 2,400 km. (1,500 miles). Bridges frequently break during the summer rainy season and snow can block passes in winter. The trip by bus or truck normally takes a week or ten days but has been known to take as long as three weeks. Travellers who have made this journey describe it as beautiful, dangerous and difficult.

Leaving Lhasa

Travellers returning by air to Chengdu are required to spend their last night in Gonggar in order to make the early morning flight. Luggage is transported from Lhasa even earlier on the day before departure, not to be seen again until arrival in Chengdu, so a separate overnight handbag is essential. Travellers flying to Golmud should also plan to sleep at Gonggar. There are two hotels.

Gonggar Hotel This newly built hotel, a short walk from the airstrip, offers approximately 50 comfortable rooms with bath and solar-heated water. It has its own restaurant.

Gonggar Guesthouse This old-fashioned guesthouse, further removed

from the airstrip, rents beds, dormitory-style, six to a room. It lacks running water or indoor toilet facilities but supplies hot water in thermoses, bedding, etc. It has a simple restaurant and a shop where food can be purchased. Rmb. 4.50 per bed per night.

Climate, Clothing and Equipment

Tibet is cold in winter, cool in summer and generally dry, receiving only 45 cm. (18 inches) of rain or snow annually. Temperatures can vary greatly within a day, however, passing 29°C (85°F) in desert areas in summer, and plunging below 4°C (40°F) at night. The higher you go the colder it gets, of course. Sunlight is extremely intense. Winds in winter are ferocious. Rainfall in southern Tibet occurs intermittently between June and September, bringing moisture to barley fields and greenery to the valleys. The pleasantest months for tourism are April to October.

Clothing should be simple and consist of layers which can be added or removed as temperatures vary during a day. A warm windbreaker and stout, comfortable shoes are especially recommended. Formal attire such as a necktie or dress is never needed — slacks and sweaters are the style.

Special items to bring to Tibet include sunscreen lotion and sunglasses as protection against the intense sunlight, a salve for the lips and a hat; any personal medicines including aspirin, as pharmacies do not exist in Lhasa; a flashlight because many interesting sights are poorly lit; and a can opener. Hikers and visitors planning to use cheap accommodation should bring toilet paper and soap. Do not bring small gifts to hand around, as this has started many children begging.

Altitude and Health

No special inoculations are required but because of Tibet's high altitude travellers with a pre-existing problem of heart, lungs or anaemia should consult a doctor before even thinking about a visit. Most other travellers, once they are acclimatised, rarely suffer more than mild discomfort from the altitude.

Acclimatisation is the adjustment of the human body to the diminished supply of oxygen at such altitudes. Bone marrow produces quantities of extra, new red blood cells to take oxygen from the air in amounts needed for good health, a process which may take several days. Mountain sickness (also called altitude sickness) is caused by an insufficient flow of oxygen to the brain and other vital organs. It can affect anybody above 3,000 m. (10,000 ft.).

Each person has a different tolerance for altitude which has nothing to do with age, sex, or state of fitness. One person will get a headache at 3,400 m. (11,000 ft.), another not until 5,500 m. (18,000 ft.) The symptoms of mountain sickness include headache, nausea and shortness of breath, singly or together. About half the people coming to Lhasa suffer from at least one symptom in the first two days and quickly recover. In 99% of cases, rest and two aspirins will relieve the discomfort. However, the serious — sometimes fatal — conditions of pulmonary and cerebral edema also begin with these same symptoms. If a headache does not respond to aspirin and a good night's rest, or if a dry cough with frothy sputum develops, or if there are any signs of severe lethargy or poor coordination, get to a hospital at once. Better yet, take the next plane to Chengdu. A lower altitude is the surest cure.

Over-exertion seems to contribute to mountain sickness and dehydration may be a predisposing factor. Sensible precautions should include:

— Stick to a schedule of mild activity and rest for the first two days.

— Drink plenty of fluids. One to five litres a day are recommended to maintain a clear, copious urine.

— Don't smoke. If you are a chronic smoker, keep it to a minimum.

— Avoid sedatives such as sleeping medicine or tranquillisers. They tend to depress respiration and limit oxygen intake.

— Diamox (acetazolamide), a mild diuretic which stimulates oxygen intake, is used by doctors of the Himalayan Rescue Association in Kathmandu for climbers making sudden ascents. This is a prescription drug. One 250 mg. tablet taken on the plane from Chengdu and another at bedtime the first night in Lhasa may help to forestall discomfort for people known to be susceptible to mountain sickness. Consult a doctor.

It is not unusual to wake up at night at high altitudes gasping for breath. Don't panic! This complaint, known as "periodic breathing", is normally quite harmless, caused by a change in the control of breathing within the brain while you sleep. Normal breathing can be quickly re-established by relaxation, rhythmic deep-breathing, and the understanding that there is nothing to worry about.

In case of illness, the hospital best equipped to care for foreigners in Lhasa is the Regional Military Hospital on the west side of Sera Monastery at the end of Jiefang Bei Lu (Map, p.36-37). A doctor is always on duty.

Visas

Since China first opened its doors to tourists in 1978, the number of places that can be visited has steadily increased. Most of these cities and areas are designated "Class A" and require no more formality from a tourist than the possession of a valid entry visa into China. There are other cities and areas designated "Class B" which are open for tourism but require an Aliens' Travel Permit (luxingzheng), a kind of internal visa obtained from Public Security Bureaux. All of Tibet falls into "Class B". A travel permit for Lhasa can be obtained with no difficulty from the Public Security Bureau in Peking, Chengdu, or any other city. A permit to visit other places in Tibet outside Lhasa can only be obtained from the Public Security Bureau in Lhasa.

At present, tourist groups under CITS care and individual tourists receive different treatment from Lhasa officials. Groups receive travel permits to all the "open" areas of Tibet without question, whereas individuals can only receive permission to go from Lhasa to the Nepal border via Gyantse, Shigatse and Zhangmu, and are expected to exit into Nepal.

Transportation

In Tibet, where distances are huge, roads bad, and all gasoline is trucked in from interior China, access to vehicles is difficult and expensive. Below are the options open to travellers:

CITS For travellers in groups, China International Travel Service automatically provides a vehicle as part of the package arrangement. CITS has a fleet of 150 vehicles in Lhasa — four-wheel-drive Toyota Land Cruisers, sedans, minibuses and full-sized buses. Land Cruisers can be hired at the rate of Rmb. 1.50 per kilometre, and minibuses that hold ten people at the rate of Rmb. 2.50 per kilometre. Every vehicle comes with a driver. Rates remain the same for long or short distances, but they can occasionally be negotiated downward for special reasons.

"Taxi Company" (Useful Addresses, p.202) This privately-run company has 11 vehicles of various sorts and vintages, including five jeeps and four minibuses. Prices range from Rmb. .80 per kilometre for a Chinese-made jeep to Rmb. 1.20 per kilometre for a minibus.

Lhasa Travel Service Company This fledgling company operates out of the Number 2 Municipal Guesthouse on Yanhe Dong Lu and has a small fleet of vehicles that, through negotiation, might be cheaper than CITS's. They prefer to rent vehicles on a daily basis around Lhasa rather than for long trips.

Lhasa City Transport Unit Access to this municipal company can be had through official guesthouses like Number 1 Provincial Guesthouse. Round-trip prices and special prices for week-long excursions can be worked out through the front desk. Prices are somewhat below those for CITS and the vehicles are in fairly good condition.

Snowland Hotel and Hotel Banak Shöl Each hotel has one or two stray vehicles with drivers which can be rented but, as with all private arrangements, *caveat emptor*.

In organising group excursions with fellow individual travellers there are certain pitfalls to be avoided. Pay only half (or less) of the total fee for a deposit to reserve the vehicle. Be sure that the itinerary is written out with destination and stops on the way, as well as starting and finishing dates. The driver should agree to it and, if possible, sign the document before starting.

Buses Within Tibet public bus service is limited, irregular and unreliable. Major destinations from Lhasa are Amdo via Damxung in the north; Nyingchi in the east; Shigatse via Gyantse in the southwest; Tsedang via Gonggar in the southeast. Bus tickets should be bought in person the day before departure at the Lhasa bus station (Map, p.36-37). Passengers should take their own drinking water and food supplies.

Trucks Rides on trucks and prices are negotiated with individual drivers at truck stops. Major truck stops in Lhasa are on Yanhe Dong Lu next to the Bank of China, and at the traffic circle 11km. (7 miles) west of Lhasa.

Money

Foreigners in China are often surprised to encounter two forms of currency. Common people use Renminbi ("people's currency") while foreigners are obliged to use its equivalent in Foreign Exchange Certificates (FEC) for all goods and services.

In Lhasa there are only two places where travellers' cheques or foreign money can be exchanged for FEC — the Lhasa Hotel and the Bank of China, which is located about a hundred yards down an unpaved road on the south side of Yanhe Dong Lu (Map, p.36-37). A small sign nailed to a tree on the north side of the street points the way. (Foreigners may also be approached in Lhasa to exchange FEC for Renminbi on the strictly illegal black market.)

It is quite common to receive Renminbi as change in shops or markets after making a purchase with FEC. These can be useful in towns outside Lhasa where FEC are a rarity. However, on leaving China Renminbi cannot be reconverted into foreign money whereas FEC can.

If you plan to travel around Tibet, change enough money in Lhasa before you go to cover all anticipated expenses. Ordinary banks in Tibet cannot handle foreign exchange.

Customs Regulations

Upon entering China all foreigners are required to register watches, radios, cameras or calculators in their possession. These must be accounted for on leaving.

Art objects and antiques in Tibet fall under special restrictions forbidding their export. Anything made before 1959 is considered an antique. Rugs may be bought and exported, so may the small religious objects that are sold in open markets, providing only one or two are taken as souvenirs. Customs officials have been known to confiscate jewellery or other objects if they consider that a tourist has purchased "too much".

Communications

Mail to or from any part of the world is reliable and quite fast if sent by airmail. Telegrams are easily sent from any post office (Useful Addresses, p.202). This is the surest, most commonly used form of communication within Tibet. Telephone service to anywhere is unreliable, although a promised communications satellite link from Lhasa should help to rectify some of the problems. Telex service is available in the Lhasa Hotel for guests staying there.

Language

In Lhasa, some Nepalese traders and Chinese speak English but few Tibetans do. Learning some basic Tibetan words will be useful (Tibetan Glossary, p.196). CITS (see below) can provide interpreters if necessary but most travellers manage without them.

CITS

China International Travel Service, also known as Luxingshe, is responsible for looking after foreign tourists in China. CITS offers a comprehensive service covering visas, accommodation, transport, food and sightseeing. It generally deals with group tours.

One of the most important services offered by CITS is renting vehicles (Transportation, p.33). The Lhasa branch of CITS also has more than 20 guides able to translate into English, French, German and Japanese, though the experience and ability of the guides vary considerably. As the volume of tourists grows and facilities expand, the number of interpreters is expected to double. CITS pins its hope on the new Lhasa Hotel (p.39) whose 1,000 beds make much of this expansion possible.

CITS service to individual tourists depends on available resources. Those requesting transport, a guide or meeting/departure service during peak tourist months of summer and autumn may be disappointed. The more profitable group tours take precedence. However, CITS is setting up an office to assist individuals near the CAAC office on Jiefang Lu.

Special interest tours for groups such as botanists or art historians can be arranged through CITS. Several months' advance notice is needed for visits to "closed" areas or any other unusual activities.

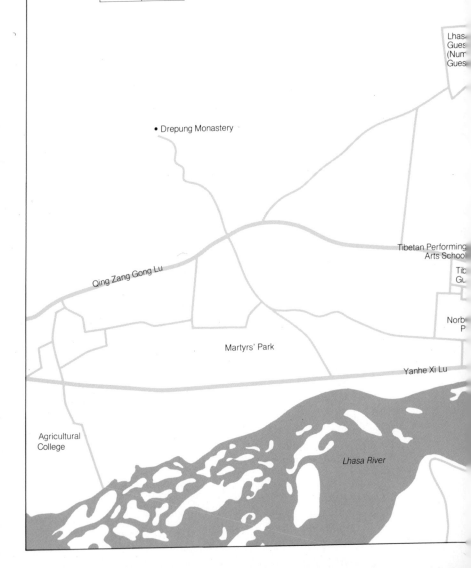

N Lhasa City

0   0.5   1 Kilometers

• Drepung Monastery

Lhas
Gues
(Nun
Gues

Tibetan Performing
Arts School

Tib
Gu

Qing Zang Gong Lu

Norb
P

Martyrs' Park

Yanhe Xi Lu

Agricultural
College

Lhasa River

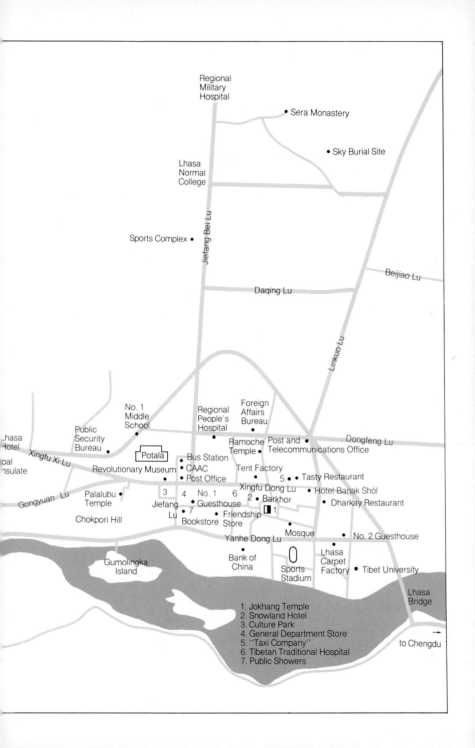

Lhasa

The city of Lhasa, population 60,000, lies in the valley of the Lhasa River, a branch of the Kyichu (Quxu) River. Its altitude is 3,607 m. (11,830 ft.). Its barren mountains average over 4,800 m. (16,000 ft.), high enough so that a night of summer rain in Lhasa can mean a ring of snowy peaks the next morning.

Two high craggy hills stand up in isolation from the valley floor. One, Red Hill, is topped by the Potala Palace, a spectacular edifice whose gold roofs soar high above the town. The other, Chokpori or Iron Hill, is crowned by a tall antenna. Chokpori, one of the four holy mountains of Central Tibet, used to be the site of a famous 17th-century monastic medical school until it was demolished by the Chinese in 1959.

Lhasa consists of two distinct parts with different architecture, population and lifestyle. Old Lhasa, the Tibetan section, centres around the Jokhang Temple, the holiest site in Tibet. Its streets are narrow, between white-washed stone houses whose walls slope inward as they rise. Windows are framed in black trapezoids, with protruding, fan-shaped eaves above. Many houses have brightly painted woodwork. The heart of Old Lhasa is the Barkhor street encircling the Jokhang. It is a sacred pilgrim path, a lively market-place and a social centre that attracts a cross-section of Tibet: traders from Kham (east Tibet) with high boots and daggers, their long hair wound in cockscombs of red yarn; shaggy nomads in sheepskins; maroon-robed monks; women twirling hand-held prayer wheels, adorned in turquoise jewellery and wearing their long hair in 108 braids — the same number as the holy sutras which pilgrims recite ecstatically at the curbside as others, covered in dust, progress by body-lengths around the Jokhang in devotional prostrations. All move in a clockwise direction as decreed by Buddhist custom. Long after the colourful shops and street stalls have closed for the night, crowds of Tibetans continue their circular walk by the light of sacred juniper fires in an atmosphere of sociability and good humour. Before 1985 the Jokhang and the Barkhor were totally hidden inside the old city. Now several blocks have been torn down to front the temple with a landscaped plaza and an avenue leading into New Lhasa.

New Lhasa, the Chinese section, was built in the last 30 years around the base of the Potala. It is characterised by straight, broad streets and utilitarian buildings that house Chinese-style department stores and all kinds of government offices. Most Chinese and some Tibetans live in "work units" — barrack-like buildings inside a walled compound with an impressive gateway. These "units" extend throughout the suburbs of New Lhasa and carry on functions ranging from foreign affairs to truck repair. A Revolutionary Museum below the Potala displays evidence of Chinese-wrought economic and social change during the past 30 years.

Lhasa underwent an unprecedented building boom in 1985 to mark the 20th anniversary of Tibet's status as an "autonomous region" inside the People's Republic of China. New Lhasa developed new streets, modern hotels and imposing public buildings. Old Lhasa saw extensive restoration of historic sites damaged in the Cultural Revolution (1966-1976) and the building of many new Tibetan-style apartment houses.

Lhasa is perhaps the only place in Asia where dogs lead a contented life. Occasional goats who still double as garbage men are not harrassed. In spite of its forced pace of modernisation Lhasa has not lost its soul. It is a friendly city where a Tibetan will always return a smile.

Hotels

Hotels in Lhasa range in size and quality from the new, modern Lhasa Hotel to very simple Tibetan inns. Prices range accordingly but there is appropriate accommodation for all budgets. Apart from the hotels where CITS puts its guests, visitors to Lhasa must be prepared for a lack of plumbing, untrained staff and various inconveniences. Nevertheless, there is a fine spirit of camaraderie among travellers and some virtue can be found in all the hotels mentioned below.

拉萨饭店　幸福西路
Lhasa Hotel (Lasa Fandian) Xingfu Xi Lu tel. 2221/23222
The Lhasa Hotel, near Norbulingka in the western suburbs, is the flagship of CITS's installations in Tibet. The first 250 rooms opened in September, 1985, with great potential. Maintenance and staff training will be the measure of the hotel's ongoing success. It will eventually accommodate 1,000 guests in double rooms with private, western-style bathrooms. It is the best equipped hotel in Tibet with a bar, two restaurants, a banquet hall and full communication services including a post office, international telephone, cable and telex. Prices up to Rmb. 100.

西藏宾馆　幸福西路
Tibet Guesthouse (Xi Zang Binguan) Xingfu Xi Lu
Nearing completion in the outer western suburbs, this neo-Tibetan-style hotel has 200 beds. All rooms have private bathrooms. While less grand than the Lhasa Hotel, by Tibetan standards it is still an up-market facility. Under Tibetan regional management, its main purpose is to accommodate top officials on tour and foreigners. Price Rmb. 80 per day.

中国国际旅行社宾馆　区三所
Lhasa CITS Guesthouse (Zhongguo Guoji Luxingshe Binguan) Qu San Suo tel. 22225

Commonly referred to as "No. 3 Guesthouse", this state-owned complex of villas and bungalows lies 10 km. (6 miles) northwest of Lhasa. It has been the lodging for CITS package tours for the past five years prior to the building of new hotels. Its major advantages are a quiet location and good food. It has seven villas where adjacent suites share a bathroom and can accommodate 150 guests. Individuals pay Rmb. 30 per bed per day.

市第二招待所　沿河东路

No. 2 Municipal Guesthouse (Shi Di Er Zhaodaisuo) Yanhe Dong Lu tel. 23196

This guesthouse, at the eastern edge of Lhasa, reserves 12 carpeted double rooms with overstuffed furniture for foreign visitors. Service desks on each floor provide fruit juice, soft drinks, beer and wine. The atmosphere is pleasant. Guests share toilets and bathroom down the hall. Price Rmb. 15 per bed per day although Lhasa Travel Service, the operator, pushes a daily package rate of Rmb. 70 including three meals. A new annex will handle many more foreign guests.

区第一招待所　人民路

No. 1 Regional Guesthouse (Qu Di Yi Zhaodaisuo) Renmin Lu tel. 22184

This guesthouse, well located between the Jokhang Temple and Potala Palace, consists of two separate units. The larger wing, west of the entrance gate, has rooms with three beds and ten-bed dormitories. One washroom with Asian-style toilets per floor has cold running water. Men and women must share the same facilities. It is often necessary to persevere at the front desk to obtain a bed and even more so to get a small room. Price Rmb. 5 per bed per day. A second building, set back in the compound, offers substantially better facilities, double rooms with cold water bathrooms and a few suites. A bath house with solar-heated water operates at 4 p.m. every day except Sunday on the third floor of the east wing. Tubs and showers can be had by buying bath tickets for Rmb. 1.50 at the front desk of the west wing. Price Rmb. 40 per bed per day. Bicycles available.

八郎学旅社　幸福东路

Hotel Banak Shöl (Balang Xue Lushe) Xingfu Dong Lu tel. 23829

This Tibetan-style hotel in the middle of Old Lhasa is built around an internal courtyard and is a favourite with young travellers. It has 44 rooms with two beds, four beds, and eight beds. It usually keeps the third floor for foreigners. There is a tap in the courtyard for washing and the latrines are fairly clean. A bath house with 24 showers is planned for the future. Price Rmb. 5 per bed per day. Bicycles available.

雪城旅馆 小花子路
Snowland Hotel (Xue Cheng Luguan) Xiao Hua Zi Lu tel. 23687
This privately operated Tibetan hotel built around an inner courtyard lies close
to the Jokhang Temple. Its 28 rooms include three doubles; others contain
four or eight beds. A pump in the courtyard provides water. Latrines are
marginal. A convivial atmosphere keeps Snowland full. Prices Rmb. 16 for
double room, Rmb. 6 per bed per day. Bicycles available.

Getting Around

Within Lhasa one of the pleasantest ways to get around is by bicycle. Most
hotels and guesthouses have bicycles to rent by the day for Rmb. 5.
However, as the demand is usually greater than the supply, it is advisable to
make a firm arrangement with the desk if you want to keep the bicycle
beyond one day. The city and the valley are flat so cycling is easy. To get
around by car, vehicles can be rented by the day or half-day from CITS
(Lhasa Hotel) or from other companies (Transportation, p.33).

Food and Drink

Traditional Tibetan cuisine consists of two basic items, salted tea mixed with
yak butter, and *tsampa*, a coarse flour made from parched barley whose
main virtues are that it is nourishing and does not need to be cooked in a
land where fuel is scarce. The tea is brewed from semi-fermented tea bricks
(a major trade item imported from Yunnan Province for well over 1,000
years) in a little water with a generous pinch of wood-ash soda, and then
placed in a churn with more boiling water, salt and yak butter. After vigorous
churning the pinkish, opaque liquid tastes more like soup than tea. Tibetans
keep it in a thermos and drink it throughout the day. Mixed with *tsampa* it
makes an edible paste. Add some dried yak meat or "dry cheese" (the
residue from boiled buttermilk) and it is a meal.

    Nowadays the diet in towns has greatly improved due to the introduction
of Chinese foods. Rice, fruit, soybean products and locally grown fresh
vegetables are commonly found. Fish, which was always abundant in Tibet's
lakes and rivers but rarely eaten, is now a growing food item. Restaurants
have proliferated in Lhasa since the end of 1984. Tinned meat, fruit and
vegetables as well as cakes, biscuits and bread can be bought in several stores
along Renmin Lu and Xingfu Dong Lu. Moslem restaurants also sell steamed
bread. One of the best diet supplements is fresh yoghurt, peddled in glass jars
along the Barkhor every morning.

    Teashops in Old Lhasa serve sweet "milk tea". The favourite local drink,
after tea, is *chang*, a greyish, flat, sour, not unpleasant barley beer. Chinese
beer in litre bottles is available in most restaurants. Imported beer and tinned

soft drinks can be bought for FEC on the top floor of the Friendship Shop (Map, pp. 36-37) and at the Lhasa Hotel. Local soft drinks are sold in stalls along the main streets.

Restaurants

Tibet is definitely not a gourmet region. Restaurant menus are limited and even listed dishes are often unavailable. Variety in vegetables is determined by Tibet's short growing season and the produce that happens to get trucked in from neighbouring Sichuan and Gansu. Meat tends to be tough, chicken is scarce, but fish, if well cooked, can be a delicious source of protein. Nearly all restaurants in Lhasa have opened only recently. By most standards they lack hygiene, atmosphere and decor. If you do not speak Chinese or Tibetan, you can feel free to go into the kitchen, look over the food and point out what you want to have cooked for your meal.

兴隆饭店　林廓路
Dharkay Restaurant (Xinglong Fandian) Linkuo Lu
Mr. Liu, the sensible Sichuanese proprietor, has made this the most successful privately run restaurant in Lhasa. His Tibetan wife and extended family all take part in the enterprise. The Dharkay, situated within two blocks of the Hotel Banak Shöl, is accustomed to foreigners. It offers a Sichuan-style menu, fish and vegetarian dishes including bean sprouts and *tofu*. It also serves a good breakfast of eggs, doughnuts and tea. It is hard to go wrong here. Prices are reasonable. Hours 9 a.m. to midnight.

美味鲜饭店　幸福东路
Tasty Restaurant (Meiweixian Fandian) Xingfu Dong Lu
This largish restaurant is well known to travellers for its good-natured staff (when it is not too crowded) and its "open kitchen" where customers can freely pick out their own menu. Meat, eggs and vegetables often run out by the end of the day, so it is better to go early. The food is standard stir-fried Chinese fare with rice as a staple. Beer can be purchased at the counter or you can bring your own drinks. As in most restaurants, beggars loiter expectantly, waiting for leftovers. (This seems to be a feature of restaurant life in Lhasa.) Prices are reasonable.

八郎学旅社饭店　幸福东路
Hotel Banak Shöl (Balang Xue Lushe Fandian) Xingfu Dong Lu
This little restaurant, entered through the kitchen from the hotel courtyard, is very informal. Customers choose from a dozen chopped, raw ingredients and wait in line for the cook to stir-fry them according to their desires. There is occasionally excellent flat bread baked on the premises. The noodles are

inedible and the rice hit or miss. The price you pay depends on a whimsical estimate by the cook but is usually reasonable.

雪城旅馆饭店　小花子路
Snowland Hotel (Xue Cheng Luguan Fandian) Xiao Hua Zi Lu
A large and relatively clean restaurant, favoured more by Chinese than Tibetans. Offers good quality Chinese fare with plenty of vegetables. Beer is available. Prices are reasonable.

拉萨饭店　幸福西路
Lhasa Hotel (Lasa Fandian) Xingfu Xi Lu
The restaurants here are well worth trying for large dishes because of the priority given to this hotel for all foodstuffs. A semblance of western food can also be found here.

中国国际旅行社宾馆　区三所
Lhasa CITS Guesthouse (Zhongguo Guoji Luxingshe Binguan) Qu San Suo
For Rmb. 15 per person you can be assured of a good variety of well-cooked Chinese dishes and all the beer you can consume.

区第一招待所　人民路
No. 1 Regional Guesthouse (West Wing) (Qu Di Yi Zhaodaisuo) Renmin Lu
If you don't mind bad service and deplorably lumpy rice, this dining hall provides plenty of adequate, cheap food on a fixed menu. The soups are generally nutritious and good. Meal tickets must be purchased in advance for Rmb. 2 at the front desk.

Moslem Restaurants

Since 1984, Lhasa's Moslems, both indigenous Tibetans and recent arrivals from Qinghai, Gansu and Ningxia, have opened a number of halal eating houses. Blue and white banners written in Chinese (and sometimes Arabic) indicate their location. The fare is simple, predictable and reliable: noodles with beef or *tofu* in broth garnished with scallions, steamed bread and good aromatic tea. The tea — green, sweetened with rock sugar and flavoured with dried fruit — is worth a stop. The standard menu can be supplemented with seeds, peanuts or canned food usually available at the counter. Half-a-dozen Moslem restaurants can be found in Old Lhasa's Moslem quarter (p.92), such as the **Qinghai**, on a wide street near the mosque. Others elsewhere include the **Qingzhen Chuncheng**, on the Barkhor and the **Halal Restaurant** on Xingfu Dong Lu.

Shopping

In the midst of Tibet's fantastic sights it may seem mundane to talk about shopping. But, in fact, there are many odd, fascinating and beautiful things to buy. Tibet's culture continues to produce all sorts of unusual objects for religious and other uses.

The best market-place for curios exists on and around the Barkhor, in the heart of Old Lhasa. Small shops carry colourful items like prayerflags, fur hats, horse bells and bridles, broad leather money-belts and copper teapots. The merchandise in small, open, street stalls changes from day to day. A curio-seeker can find temple bells, conch-shell trumpets, rosaries, prayer wheels, amulets and a variety of turquoise, coral and silver jewellery — alongside dayglo socks and plastic shoes!

Tibetan rugs can be found hanging on display along the Barkhor. Some of these have more individuality and aesthetic appeal than the rugs produced for export in the Lhasa Carpet Factory (p.96). As you amble clockwise around the Jokhang Temple you will invariably be approached by Tibetan pilgrim-traders, eager to sell you their own swords, inlaid knives, jewellery, Buddha figures and who knows what else.

In the Barkhor's shops and stalls, and above all with individuals, you must bargain. As a loose guideline, you might get prices in shops down 20%-25%, but from stalls and individuals you should get nearer 50%. Haggling is a game which every Tibetan enjoys and it should be played with perseverance, patience and good humour. However, remember that the purchase of too many souvenir "cultural objects" may invite confiscation by customs officials when you leave the country.

For those who prefer fixed prices, a fair variety of Tibetan handicrafts is on sale at the "Selling Department for Tourist Products" on Xingfu Dong Lu (Useful Addresses, p.202).

Any visitor to Lhasa notices the decorated tents, canopies and awnings which Tibetans use for numerous outdoor purposes. These are becoming a popular item for travellers to take home. At the Lhasa Tent and Banner Factory (Useful Addresses, p.202) skilled artisans can copy and custom-make any design they are presented with. A 4m. X 3m. white canopy with blue appliquéd symbols costs about Rmb. 55. A four-sided family tent in three colours with bestiary appliqué decorations costs approximately Rmb. 250.

If you need to buy practical items for everyday use, there are two main department stores in New Lhasa. The General Department Store is a rambling, cavernous, L-shaped store on the corner of Renmin Lu and Jiefang Lu and the Nong Ken Ting Department Store is a partly empty, multi-storey building (with the Friendship Store on its top floor) halfway along the south side of Renmin Lu. (Map, p.36-37). At these shops you can buy good, comfortable, cotton clothing, canteens, mugs, canned food, writing paper and envelopes, soap, towels, toothpaste, etc. If you're lucky, toilet paper can be found in the Nong Ken Ting's side-street, tinned food section.

Lhasa's major bookshop, Xinhua Shudian on Renmin Lu, is not impressive but it does carry maps of Lhasa, posters, Tibetan primers and Tibetan-Chinese dictionaries, plus Chinese and Tibetan paperback books. A Tibetan bookshop with similar literature is located just north of the Barkhor, west of the meat market.

Traditional Tibetan Carpet

Explorers, Characters and Cranks

Tibet exerted a magnetic pull upon western travellers for over 100 years largely because it was forbidden. Intrepid, foolhardy, serious, determined, they tried to reach Lhasa by every conceivable means — and most failed. They were spies, missionaries, scholars, geographers, mystics, soldiers, cranks, and their true stories put fiction to shame.

Tibet was not always forbidden to foreigners. The first Europeans to arrive were Portuguese missionaries in 1624. They were amiably received by the Tibetans and allowed to build a church. The next century brought more Jesuits and Capuchins from Europe who met opposition from Tibet's lamas and they were finally expelled in 1745. However, the hard feelings were not directed against foreigners as such. In 1774, George Bogle, an Englishman, came to Shigatse to investigate trade for the British East India Company. He not only befriended the Panchen Lama but ended up marrying a Tibetan and introducing the first potatoes into Tibet.

The 19th century grew ominous. The British Empire was encroaching north from India into the Himalayas and Afghanistan. The Russian Empire of the Tsars was expanding south into Central Asia. Each power suspected that the other had designs on Tibet, about which almost nothing was known. China, which claimed Tibet as a protectorate, fanned Tibet's fears that foreigners threatened its gold fields and its religion. Tibet's answer was to clamp shut its borders, except to China. Mutilation, torture and death awaited any Tibetan who even unwittingly gave assistance to a foreigner.

In 1865, the British started secretly mapping Tibet. Trained Indian surveyor-spies disguised as pilgrims or traders counted their strides on rosaries clear across Tibet and took readings at night. Nain Singh, the most famous, measured the longitude, latitude and altitude of Lhasa, and traced the Yarlong Tsangpo River far westward without being discovered.

Seven years later, Nicholas Przewalski, a great Russian explorer and colonel in the Tsar's army, entered Tibet from the north. He gathered much scientific information, but in three tries he never reached Lhasa. In spite of his Cossack escort and his reputation among simple Tibetans as a wizard, the terrain and official stubbornness defeated him.

From then on until the end of the century many tried their luck for many reasons — to write a bestseller, explore the unknown, become famous, fulfil a dream. Tales of incredible hardship, ferocious weather, bandits and intransigent monk-officials accompanied all those who returned.

The first American to try the trek to Lhasa was William Rockhill, a young diplomat in Peking, in 1889. Disguised as a Mongolian, speaking Tibetan and Chinese, he failed because his guides deserted him in the vast uninhabited wasteland. Two years later he tried again and was repelled only 177 km. (110 miles) from Lhasa. But he brought back much knowledge.

In 1892, Annie Taylor, a frail English missionary, became the first European woman to approach Lhasa. She came within three days' march of it. Armed only with indomitable faith and fearlessness, she survived bandits, betrayal, illness and exposure. When finally caught, she out-talked her Tibetan judge and saved her life.

In 1895, Mr. St. G. Littledale, an English gentleman and veteran of two previous Central Asian explorations, set out for Lhasa with his wife, nephew and little dog, Tanny. The small band braved blizzards; servants deserted; pack animals died. Fearing detection, they travelled by night. Finally stopped by 500 armed Tibetans only 79 km. (49 miles) from Lhasa, neither a proffered bribe nor Mrs. Littledale's declaration that she was Queen Victoria's sister could save them from expulsion. But the Royal Geographical Society awarded Mr. Littledale its gold medal and Tanny was made an Honorary Fellow with a silver collar.

The 20th century opened with violence. British India was frustrated by murky relations with Tibet and afraid Tibet might bestow its favours on Russia. In 1904, a military expedition led by Colonel Francis Younghusband (p.123) forced its way to Lhasa, leaving hundreds of Tibetan soldiers dead. After imposing a treaty, it withdrew. The British wanted Tibet to remain closed to all foreigners but themselves. (Sir Charles Bell, the political officer for Tibet, became a profound scholar of Tibetology and a close friend and advisor to the Thirteenth Dalai Lama.)

Nevertheless, others came. Sven Hedin, a peerless Swedish explorer, defied the British and continued his decade-long work of quietly mapping western and southern Tibet. Alexandra David-Neel, a French Buddhist scholar and mystic, reached Shigatse where she was ordained by the Panchen Lama. Later, aged 53, disguised as a beggar, she became the first European woman to reach Lhasa. Giuseppe Tucci, an Italian archaeologist, began a 20-year study of Tibet in 1927, travelling thousands of miles on foot, to produce some of the definitive books on Tibetan religion and culture.

At the start of the Second World War, two Austrian mountaineers in the Himalayas became prisoners-of-war in British India. Heinrich Harrer and his companion escaped into Tibet and miraculously reached Lhasa, where Harrer eventually served as the young Dalai Lama's tutor. His book, *Seven Years In Tibet*, written after the war, aroused great interest in Tibet. The Dalai Lama shrewdly invited well-known American commentators, Lowell Thomas and Lowell Thomas, Jr., to visit Tibet in 1949. As he hoped, their films created world-wide sympathy and good will towards his exotic land.

After 1951, the Chinese invited hand-picked foreign journalists to report favourably about the changes going on, but with minimal effect. Now Tibet is open to all foreigners and their tales and photographs, more than anything else, will keep the world well informed about Tibet.

Sights

Background The greatest sights around Lhasa proclaim Tibet's unique past, which has been the story of a religion rather than that of a nation. The Tibetan people and their religion are inseparable.

Their origin is myth. Long ago, they believe, the Bodhisattva of Compassion, Chenrezi, sent his disciple, a holy monkey, to be a hermit in the mountains. Meditating in his cave, the monkey heard an ogress crying among the crags and took pity on her loneliness. (Some say she threatened to marry a demon and people the world with their offspring.) In either case, the monkey got Chenrezi's permission to marry the ogress. In due time they had six children who grew up to be human beings with noble traits from their father such as generosity, bravery and piety, and base ones from their mother like greed, envy and lust. They multiplied and became the Tibetan people, whose first kings descended from the sky. The Tibetans practised Bon, a faith filled with demons and magic.

Recorded history begins with the reign of King Songtsen Gampo (608-650 AD), a young warrior king who unified all Tibet and made Lhasa his capital. He posed enough threat to China that he could demand a Chinese princess as a bride. The Emperor Tai Zong, first of the Tang Dynasty, sent his adopted daughter, Wen Cheng, to Tibet with pomp and ceremony, and a gold Buddha statue as her dowry. Songtsen Gampo made another alliance by marrying Princess Tritsun from Nepal. His three Tibetan wives gave birth to the children who founded Tibet's Tubo Dynasty.

The two foreign princesses, both Buddhists, converted the king from the Bon faith to Buddhism and persuaded him to wear silk instead of sheepskins. Songtsen Gampo built a fortress on Red Hill, the first Potala, for them to live in, and he built the Jokhang and Ramoche Temples in Lhasa to house their sacred Buddha statues.

The king then sent a bright young man, Sambhota, to India to learn a system of writing. He invented a Tibetan orthography based on that of Kashmir and adapted its script to his complicated language — a brilliant feat. Ancient annals show that within 20 years it was widely used in Tibet to write documents and laws, as well as write translations of Buddhist texts. Much later, when lamas ruled Tibet, Songtsen Gampo, the first "Religious King", was declared to be an incarnation of Chenrezi, the Bodhisattva of Compassion, and the patron saint of Tibet. His image is frequently seen in temples (p.58).

After Songtsen Gampo, four generations of kings devoted themselves to wars of conquest. Buddhism made headway by absorbing many features of the old Bon faith and also of Indian Tantrism — a branch of Buddhism that included esoteric and sexual elements, and paranormal powers. This three-fold mixture is sometimes called Lamaism. A lama was a highly learned

monk but although a lama had to be a monk, relatively few monks became lamas.

The second great king of the Tubo line was Trisong Detsen (755-797).Like his ancestor Songtsen Gampo he was a notable military commander. His armies campaigned from Samarkand to Chang'an, the capital of China. But he is best remembered for his role as Tibet's second "Religious King" who definitively rooted Buddhism in Tibet. Trisong Detsen called in famous Buddhist teachers from India and China, among them a great Indian Tantric mystic named Padmasambhava, who so terrified the Bon priests that they eventually forced him to leave. Padmasambhava had a far-reaching influence and became the patron saint of early Lamaism. His image can be seen in many temples and monasteries (p.58).

Trisong Detsen founded Samye, Tibet's first monastery, in 779 (p.130) where Tibetans could be trained as monks. When fundamental conflicts appeared between the doctrines of India and China, the king staged public debates at Samye between the masters of both schools of thought. The Indians won hands down. Thereafter, Indian philosophy held sway in Tibet, although some elements of Chinese Chan Buddhism did enter Lamaism.

During Trisong Detsen's reign, the influence of monks on Tibetan life began to grow. It reached its climax 50 years later when his grandson turned over his whole administration to a monk. That blindly pious king was assassinated and his brother, Lang Darma, seized the throne. Lang Darma (reigned 836-842) set out to extinguish Buddhism. Monasteries were systematically disbanded, monks were persecuted, and religion in Tibet went into eclipse for more than 100 years. Lang Darma himself was murdered by an avenging monk and with that the monarchy came to an end. Tibet collapsed into enclaves ruled by rival clans.

Gradually, peace returned and Buddhism trickled back. In 1042, a famous Tantric master from India, named Atisha, journeyed northward just when Tibet was ready for a religious revival. Under his influence Tibetans formed communities to study aspects of Lamaist doctrine. Thus arose the sects, known by the colour of their hats, which fought for control of Tibet during the next 500 years. "Red Hats" and "Black Hats" were the strongest.

New monasteries were founded at this time, the greatest of which was Sakya (p.160). When Genghis Khan, the Mongol tyrant, forced Tibet into submission, Sakya's abbot converted the Mongols to Buddhism. The next abbot, Phagspa, went to Peking as mentor to Kublai Khan, the emperor. (Phagspa's diary mentions meeting Marco Polo there.) As a favour, the Emperor granted Sakya Monastery the right to rule Tibet in 1254. Rival sects resented this privilege. After 90 years, other monasteries, with princely Tibetan patrons, seized control and kept on wrangling for power.

Into this mess came a saintly scholar named Tsong Khapa (1357-1419), Tibet's great reformer. He founded Ganden Monastery near Lhasa, and began a new sect, the "Yellow Hats". Strict morality, celibacy, and a purified doctrine that followed Atisha's teachings marked the Yellow Hat monks. Tsong Khapa's disciples founded Lhasa's huge monasteries of Sera and Drepung and popularised their master's theological writings. The Yellow Hat sect eventually became Tibet's state religion. The image of Tsong Khapa, its founder, appears in temples and monasteries almost as frequently as the Buddha's (p.58).

One line of Yellow Hat abbots were known as Dalai Lamas (p.68). They had equal status with high lamas of other sects until the Fifth Dalai Lama (1617-1682) ensured their supremacy for good. With the help of a Yellow Hat Mongolian prince who supplied an army, the Great Fifth unified Tibet under his own leadership, subdued the nobility and ended any secular role for the Red or Black Hat sects. To solidify Yellow Hat control, he gave his own revered teacher the title of Panchen Lama (p.110), with spiritual powers equal to his own, and placed him in Shigatse.

The Fifth Dalai Lama built the vast Potala Palace as his centre of government. He declared all Dalai Lamas (as well as King Songtsen Gampo) to be reincarnations of Chenrezi, thus making them God-Kings. High lamas wielded great power throughout Tibet as Regents or members of ruling councils. The tax-exempt, landowning monasteries accumulated huge wealth.

An unchangeable theocracy prevailed in Tibet until 1951. The outside world was feared and shut out. No subsequent ruler approached the stature of the Great Fifth until the Thirteenth Dalai Lama (1876-1933). This able man made concerted efforts to bring Tibet into the 20th century but with scant success. When China entered Tibet in 1951, there were no public schools and no roads outside Lhasa.

The Tibetan uprising of 1959 brought fierce reprisals from the Chinese. The Dalai Lama and 80,000 followers fled. All old institutions vanished, monasteries were dismantled and Tibet was forced into a modern socialist world. Wanton destruction in the Cultural Revolution (1966-1976) wiped out much of the physical evidence of Tibet's original culture. Only 13 of a former 20,000 monasteries remained standing and many magnificent landmarks were gone for ever.

Tibet started to stir again in 1980. New policies in Peking allowed the people more religious and economic freedom. Worshippers and traders resumed their pilgrimages to Lhasa. Money was provided for the repair of famous historic buildings by Tibetan artisans under Tibetan foremen, many of them former monks, hitting a peak in 1985. Visitors to Lhasa can now recapture a few echoes of Tibet's amazing cultural past. If they keep their eyes open and are not afraid to explore, they may discover surprising corners that are not on any tourist itinerary — a hidden nunnery, a sculptor at work in a little, unmarked temple — where the religious culture is now spontaneously trying to recreate itself.

Admission Times There are few official admission times; those quoted below may therefore be subject to change.

Photography Visitors are generally allowed to take photos of sights from the outside without charge. Inside temples, in particular, each shot may be subject to a fee of about Rmb. 20 (up to Rmb. 100 in the Fifth Dalai Lama's Mausoleum), payable to the monks in charge.

The Jokhang Temple (9-1 Closed Sunday. No admission fee)

The Jokhang is the spiritual centre of Tibet, its most holy place, the destination, over time, of millions of Tibetan pilgrims.

The oldest part of the Jokhang dates from the 7th century AD. It was one of two temples built by King Songtsen Gampo to house the statues of Buddha that his two foreign wives brought to Tibet from China and Nepal. Legend says that Songtsen Gampo threw his ring into the air, promising to build a temple wherever it landed. The ring fell into a lake and struck a rock where a white stupa miraculously appeared — an auspicious sign. Workmen filled in the lake with stones and the Jokhang was built over it by craftsmen from Tibet, China, Nepal and Kashmir. Even today, a pool exists under the Jokhang's main courtyard.

Despite removal of part of the Barkhor in 1985 to make way for a plaza, three monuments that stood there can still be seen in front of the Jokhang, inside walled enclosures. The pillar on the left is a treaty stone recording an alliance between the King of Tibet and the Emperor of China in 823 AD. On the right, the more visible of the two tablets was erected by the Chinese in 1794 announcing procedures in case of a smallpox epidemic — but it was partly eaten away by people who thought the stone itself had curative powers.

The outer courtyard and porch of the temple are usually filled with pilgrims making full-length prostrations towards the holy sanctum. Its innermost shrine contains the oldest, most precious object in Tibet — the original statue of Sakyamuni (the historical Buddha), which Princess Wen Cheng brought from Chang'an 1,300 years ago, and which is considered so holy that even Red Guard vandals did not dare to harm it during the Cultural Revolution.

Layout The Jokhang was enlarged eight times between the 7th century and 1660, when the Fifth Dalai Lama added its last embellishments. It consists of an elaborate porch leading to a frescoed cloister around an open courtyard. Outside runs a long gallery of prayer wheels. A passage leads into a main hall with numerous small chapels around it. The sacred shrine holding the ancient Buddha statue is centred at the rear of this main hall. Above, another floor has historically valuable murals. At the top, a three-level roof enjoys a life of its own. Although monks have been attached to the Jokhang for centuries, its eminence rests on the sacred statuary and shrines of the temple, not on fame as a monastery.

Unlike the lofty Potala, the Jokhang has intimate, human proportions. Pilgrims inch their way clockwise towards the Holy of Holies, crowding through low chapel doorways in semi-darkness with gifts of yak butter as fuel for the myriad flickering votive lamps, or white scarves to honour the deities. The murmuring of mantras sounds like a distant swarm of bees.

The Main Hall is entered through a corridor graced by guardian statues — fierce on the left, benign on the right. Here a delightful set of murals depicts Wen Cheng's procession coming to Tibet with the statue enthroned in a horse-drawn carriage, and then the building of the Jokhang. In the middle of the hall sit two huge images of Padmasambhava (left) and Sakyamuni (right). Between them, a delicate, eleven-headed Chenrezi expresses infinite compassion. Above, beams carved as human-faced lions show Persian influence, brought in via Kashmir. Numerous small chapels enshrining a variety of Tibetan deities progress to the back wall.

The Holy of Holies may be closed off behind an iron mesh curtain. On holy days pilgrims can circumambulate the shrine. The statue, gilded many times, crowned, encrusted with jewels and placed in an elaborate setting, originally represented Sakyamuni aged 12. On both sides of the shrine are altars with images of Songtsen Gampo and his two wives (p. 58).

The Roof can only be visited with a CITS guide, for a fee, but photography is allowed. There is a splendid view over the Barkhor to the Potala. The roof is a conglomerate of pavilions, craftsmen's workshops, monks' living rooms and gold roofs that are adorned with bells, figures, birds, beasts and dragons. At the front, two golden deer holding the Buddhist "Wheel of Dharma" recall the Buddha's first sermon in a deer park.

Easily Recognised Figures

In the phantasmagoria of figures that populate
Tibetan art in sculpture, mural paintings and
thangkas, some important historical people and
religious beings can be recognised by their
iconographic conventions.

King Songtsen Gampo (608-650 AD). Introduced
Buddhism to Tibet. Founded Tubo line of kings.
Always wears high orange or gold turban with small
Chenrezi head peeping out of the top. Chinese
wife, Wen Cheng, always on viewer's right.
Nepalese wife, Tritsun, on viewer's left.

Padmasambhava (or Guru Rinpoche — 8th
century). Invited from India to Tibet 747. Exorcised
demons by supernatural powers. Founded earliest
Tibetan Buddhist sect. Wears magical, crown-like,
red hat. Severe expression, curled moustache.
Carries *dorje* (p. 90) and magic sceptre with
skull-heads.

Tsong Khapa (1357-1419). Great reformer of
Tibetan Buddhism. Founder of the Yellow Hat sect.
Always seated. Wears pointed yellow cap with long
ear flaps. Usually smiling, with a bulbous nose. His
image is often repeated with large and small
versions of himself sitting side by side.

Fifth Dalai Lama (1617-1682). Greatest of all
Dalai Lamas. Unified Tibet and made Yellow Hat
sect the state religion. Built the Potala. Wears
pointed yellow cap with ear flaps. Portly, with
double chins and popping eyes. Often has small
moustache.

Sakyamuni (5th century BC). The historical Buddha (p.138). His Enlightenment and teachings set in motion the Buddhist faith, claiming 300 million followers today. Often has blue hair with a cranial bump on top, but sometimes crowned. Always sits cross-legged on a lotus flower throne.

Chenrezi, the Bodhisattva of Compassion. (Tibetan manifestation of India's Avalokitesvara, China's Guan Yin.) In full splendour he displays 11 heads (of which one is wrathful) and multiple pairs of arms. Sometimes encircled by 1,000 hands. In simpler forms he is hard to distinguish from other crowned Buddhas.

Tara, the most beloved of female deities. Special proctectress and saviour of the Tibetan people. Symbolises fertility. Believed to fulfil wishes. Green Tara associated with night and Tritsun, White Tara with day and Wen Cheng. Usually seated. Wears pagoda-shaped crown. Delicate features. Has seven eyes, on face, hands and feet.

Yamantaka the Terrible. Favourite of the Eight Guardians of the Faith, popularised by Tsong Khapa. A wrathful form of the Bodhisattva of Wisdom. Coloured blue with horned bull's head. Many arms. Body draped with skulls. Tramples on human forms representing stupidity, sloth and nihilism. Often shown in a sexual embrace (*yab-yum*) with his female partner, Prajna (Wisdom), symbolising the union of compassion and insight.

Four Heavenly Kings, Guardians of the Four Directions. Usually found as large statues or murals in temple porches and entrances. East is white, carries a musical instrument. South is blue, carries a sword. West is red, usually carries a stupa or *dorje*. North is orange and carries an umbrella. The chief of the Four Kings is East.

The Potala (9-4 Closed Sunday. Some parts are locked 12:30-2:30. Admission Rmb. .30)

This architectural wonder of the world is built on the escarpments of Red Hill and rises more than 300 m. (1,000 ft.) above the valley floor. The awesome Potala can be seen from all directions for miles around.

A stronghold probably existed on Red Hill as early as the 7th century AD when King Songtsen Gampo built a fortress on it for his two foreign wives. He is reputed to have studied the Buddhist scriptures there after his conversion from the Bon faith. Fires, lightning and wars took their toll, yet 1,000 years later, two of the original rooms still remained.

The present Potala was built mainly in the Fifth Dalai Lama's reign, between 1645 and 1693. It became the winter palace in 1755 when the Seventh Dalai Lama made the Norbulingka into a summer residence. The Potala remained the centre of political and religious power for the Dalai Lamas.

With over 1,000 rooms, it contained the living quarters of the Dalai Lamas while they lived, and their sumptuous golden tombs when they died. Regents, tutors and other high lamas had apartments in the palace, too. The Potala held the offices of government, a huge printing house where Buddhist scriptures were hand-printed from woodblocks, and a seminary run by the elite order of monks who surrounded the God-King to train government officials. Hundreds of elaborately decorated chapels and shrines, halls and corridors contained thousands of gilded statues — Tibet's pantheon of Buddhas, Bodhisattvas, saints and demons. The round, outside towers were fortifications. A legend says they are wings which will fly the Potala to safety from a future, devastating flood.

Beneath the splendid ceremonial areas of the palace lay a warren of soot-blackened cells for monks and servants, and two great treasuries — one for the Dalai Lamas and Regents, and one for the state. Still lower lay granaries and storerooms filled with pilgrims' gifts and enough yak butter to burn for years in the Potala's countless votive lamps. At the base, carved from living rock, were the dungeons, the dreaded Cave of Scorpions, from which enemies of the rulers rarely emerged.

Today the Potala is a state museum with 35 caretaker monks, but to many thousands of Tibetan pilgrims it remains a beloved shrine. Visitors should respect Buddhist custom by moving in a clockwise direction around the rooms wherever possible.

Layout The Potala consists of a White and a Red Palace, with one small yellow portion between. The first White Palace was built in the lifetime of the Fifth Dalai Lama, then extended to its present size by the Thirteenth Dalai Lama in the early 20th century. The Great Fifth moved to the Potala from Drepung Monastery in about 1650. His death in 1682 was concealed for ten years by the Regent, who explained his absence as a series of religious retreats. During those years the Red Palace was built.

The White Palace was for secular uses. It contained living quarters, offices, the seminary and the printing house. The Red Palace's function was religious. It contained gold stupas (p.121), which were the tombs of eight Dalai Lamas, the monks' assembly hall, numerous chapels and shrines, and libraries for Buddhist scriptures: the *Kanjur* with 108 volumes, and the *Tenjur* with 225. The yellow building between the main palaces housed giant banners embroidered with holy symbols which hung across the south face of the Potala during New Year festivals.

Construction of the Potala was a huge undertaking. It is 13 storeys high, measuring 400 m. (1,312 ft.) east-west and 350 m. (1,148 ft.) north-south. Its inward-sloping stone walls are 5 m. (over 16 ft.) thick at the base and average 3 m. (9 ft.). Copper was poured into the foundations to help withstand earthquakes. So much earth was dug up for mortar behind Red Hill that the pit was turned into a lake. (The flighty Sixth Dalai Lama later added a pavilion in the middle of it for his dalliances.)

Upper parts of the Potala have such finely joined wooden brackets, beams and eaves that no nails were needed. The upper exterior walls are made from twigs tightly rammed end-in and painted brownish-red — a uniquely Tibetan style reserved for sacred buildings and houses of nobles in high authority. The roofs are made of gilded copper. Murals in the Red Palace's lower gallery show the building of the Potala in splendid detail.

Tour groups are brought by bus up Red Hill to enter the Red Palace at the western end. Individuals and pilgrims approach through Sho, a village at the base of Red Hill formerly enclosed within the Potala's compound wall. A steep climb up the main east-central flight of steps leads to the eastern portal of the White Palace. The approaches to both entrances are decorated with *mani* stones (p.90), small cairns, prayer flags and knotted garlands of yak hair left by pilgrims as devotional offerings.

Only a relatively small part of the Potala is open to the public but it is still easy to get lost. It is useful to bring a flashlight.

The White Palace The central yellow-painted courtyard, or Deyangshar, is reached from the East Portal by a broad corridor that climbs upward between thick walls to an entrance with hanging drums. The large, open court is surrounded by a two-storey gallery of rooms (former offices) embellished with sacred emblems (p.78.) On the west side is the exterior of the Dalai Lama's living quarters, from whose upper windows the God-King would watch religious ceremonies and performances below. On the east is Tsedrung seminary (left) and its dormitory (right). A souvenir shop and tour guide office are located on the north side.

The Roof is reached by a series of ladder-stairs from the west side of the courtyard. The first hallway contains an edict of the Fifth Dalai Lama, copied

from the original and signed with the Thirteenth Dalai Lama's handprint. Opposite, murals depict construction in the 7th century AD. The flat roof has some fine examples of the golden roof ornaments and finials that are typical of Tibetan religious architecture. There is also an unsurpassed view of the Lhasa valley. Heinrich Harrer (p.46) tells how, in the 1940s, the teenaged Dalai Lama set up a brass telescope here and escaped his lonely God-King's life by watching the common people.

The Apartments on the east side of the roof belonged to the Thirteenth and Fourteenth Dalai Lamas. The Chamber of Eastern Light, with a throne and library, overlooks the main courtyard. Proceeding clockwise through formal living rooms, one reaches the suite of the present Dalai Lama who is now in India. The innermost room contains his yellow iron bed and personal belongings, such as a clock and calendar, left almost exactly as they were on the day of his departure.

From the west side of the roof, a chapel with a giant Maitreya statue gives entry to the Sixth Dalai Lama's chanting hall and formal rooms. A corridor beyond leads to the Red Palace through a hall that houses the tombs of the Seventh, Eighth and Ninth Dalai Lamas behind red doors with gold grills. Here, too, sits a statue of the Sixth. He has no tomb because he disappeared, aged 23, after being kidnapped (p.68).

The Saint's Chapel, on the north side of this hall, is the Potala's holiest shrine. A big gold and blue inscription over the door was written by the 19th-century Chinese Emperor Tong Zhi, proclaiming Buddhism a "Blessed Field of Wonderful Fruit". This chapel, like the Dharma Cave below it, dates from the 7th century. It contains a small, ancient, jewel-encrusted statue of Chenrezi with two attendants. On the floor below, a low, dark passage leads into the Dharma Cave where Songtsen Gampo is believed to have studied Buddhism. Here are images of Songtsen Gampo, his wives, his chief minister and Sambhota, the scholar who developed Tibetan writing, in the company of many divinities.

The Red Palace The layout is complicated. Its centre is the Great West Hall with four large chapels. Light comes in from a free-standing pavilion built directly overhead, around which are three levels of open galleries like a hollow square. Chapels open off these galleries.

The Great West Hall and its chapels proclaim the glory and power of the Fifth Dalai Lama. The Hall is noted for its fine murals, reminiscent of Persian miniatures, depicting events in the Fifth Dalai Lama's life. The famous scene of his visit to Emperor Shun Zhi in Peking is located on the east wall just outside the entrance. Special cloth from Bhutan wraps the Hall's numerous columns. Four important chapels open off the Great West Hall, which should be visited in clockwise sequence.

The North Chapel (where tour groups enter) centres on a crowned Sakyamuni Buddha (left) and the Fifth Dalai Lama (right), seated on magnificent gold thrones. Their equal height and shared aura imply equal status. Far left is the gold stupa tomb of the Eleventh Dalai Lama who died as a child, with two rows of benign Medicine Buddhas, the heavenly healers. On the right are Chenrezi and his historical incarnations, including Songtsen Gampo and the first four Dalai Lamas. Scriptures (loose leaves wrapped in silk between wooden covers) form a pigeonhole library.

The East Chapel is dedicated to Tsong Khapa, founder of the Yellow Hat sect. His central figure is surrounded by lamas from Sakya Monastery who had briefly ruled Tibet and formed their own sect until converted by Tsong Khapa. Other statues include the alert-looking Dalai Lamas.

The South Chapel centres on Padmasambhava, the 8th-century Indian magician-saint (p.58). His Tibetan wife, a gift from the king, is by his left knee; his wife from his native land of Swat is by his right knee. Left, eight of his holy manifestations meditate with inturned gaze. Right, eight wrathful manifestations wield instruments of magic power to subdue demons of the Bon faith. Beautiful thangkas (p.70) hang above.

The West Chapel contains five golden stupas. The gigantic central one contains the mummified body of the Fifth Dalai Lama. This stupa, built of sandalwood, is coated with 3,727 kg. (8,200 lb.) of gold "as thick as a cow's hide" and studded with semi-precious jewels. It rises for more than three storeys, 14.8 m. (48 1/2 ft.) high. On the left is the funeral stupa of the Twelfth Dalai Lama, and on the right that of the Tenth. The stupas on both ends contain scriptures.

On the floor above, **The First Gallery** has windows that give light and ventilation to the Great West Hall and chapels below. Between the windows, superb murals show the Potala's construction in fine detail.

The Second Gallery gives access to the central pavilion for a rest, a cup of tea and a chance to buy souvenirs. This gallery also has excellent murals with scenes from Tibetan history.

The Third Gallery, besides fine murals, has dark rooms containing "Bronze Heavens", full of miniature figures in brass, copper and gold. Take your flashlight! The Seventh Dalai Lama's chanting hall and apartment are on the south side. On the east, an entrance connects with the Saint's Chapel, and on to the White Palace.

A trip to **The Thirteenth Dalai Lama's Tomb** must be in company with a monk and a Potala guide (none of whom speak foreign languages) or a CITS guide. Located west of the Great West Hall, it can only be reached from an upper floor. Built in 1933, the giant stupa contains priceless jewels and a ton of gold. It is 14 m. (46 ft.) high. Devotional offerings include elephant tusks from India, porcelain lions and vases, and a pagoda made of 200,000 pearls. Elaborate murals in traditional style show many events from the Thirteenth Dalai Lama's life in the 20th century.

The Dalai Lamas

"Dalai Lama" was the title of Tibet's rulers for over 500 years. Fourteen Dalai Lamas ruled in succession, each one a reincarnation of his predecessor, according to Tibetan belief. The title "Dalai", or "Ocean" (presumably "ocean of wisdom") was given to the Third in 1578 by a Mongol king, and applied posthumously to the first two. The Fifth named himself, his four predecessors and all future Dalai Lamas as incarnations of the Bodhisattva of Compassion, Chenrezi, thus adopting divine status.

When a Dalai Lama died, a search for his reincarnation began at once. Helped by the State Oracle, portents and dreams, high lamas scoured Tibet for a boy with special physical traits, like big ears and long eyes, who, in addition to other tests, could identify the late Dalai Lama's possessions among a pile of similar objects. In case of rival candidates, they drew lots. Until the new Dalai Lama was 18, a Regent wielded unlimited power. The Fifth and Thirteenth were the greatest Dalai Lamas.

The First Dalai Lama (1391-1474) was a disciple of Tsong Khapa. He founded Tashilhunpo Monastery, at Shigatse, and was its first abbot.

The Second (1475-1542) served as the abbot of three great Yellow Hat monasteries while disputes raged between rival Tibetan sects.

The Third (1543-1588), an abbot of Drepung Monastery, succeeded in reviving Buddhism in Mongolia. Altan Khan, the king, became his patron.

The Fourth (1588-1616) was conveniently discovered to be the great-grandson of Altan Khan — the only non-Tibetan in the line of Dalai Lamas.

The Great Fifth (1617-1682) was a mighty scholar, politician and architect. Aided by a Mongol prince, he unified Tibet under his rule and suppressed all rivals of the Yellow Hat sect. The Potala is his monument.

The Sixth (1683-1706) preferred women, wine and poetry to duty. Angry Mongolians killed the Regent and kidnapped him. He was never seen again.

The Seventh (1708-1757) was installed with Chinese help after Mongols imposed a false Dalai Lama. Until 1912 Tibet was a protectorate of China.

The Eighth through Twelfth (1758-1875) are of minor importance. Most died young (probably poisoned) while their Regents held on to power.

The Great Thirteenth (1876-1933) withstood a British invasion in 1904 and made Tibet independent in 1912 after China became a republic. An able, intelligent ruler, he tried in vain to modernise Tibet's institutions.

The Fourteenth (b. 1935) was only 16 when Mao Zedong's China took over Tibet. He ruled in partial capacity under the Chinese for ten years but in 1959 fled, with 80,000 followers, to India where he keeps an active headquarters. He is still held in great esteem in Tibet.

The First Dalai Lama is entombed at Tashilhunpo Monastery; the Second, Third and Fourth at Drepung Monastery; and all the others (except the Sixth, who has no tomb) inside the Potala.

Thangkas

Thangka is the name for the scroll-banners seen hanging in every temple, monastery and family shrine in Tibet. They carry painted or embroidered pictures inside a broad, coloured border and they can range in size from the page of a book to the facade of an entire building. The picture is usually made on paper or cotton canvas which is protected by a thin dust-cover; the mounting is of colourful silk. A heavy wooden stick at the base allows a thangka to be rolled up like a scroll for storage or transportation, or to hang securely without flapping.

Thangkas first appeared in Tibet around the 10th century AD. The scroll form seems to have been borrowed from China; the style of painting probably came from Nepal and Kashmir. Apprentice thangka painters studied under experienced lamas and their works were consecrated before they could be hung.

Thangkas were widely used in monastery schools as teaching tools because of their convenient movability. Common folk hung them in homes as protection against evil spirits. At the highest level of religious practice, mystics in a state of meditation would become one with the deity portrayed.

Thangkas can be simple in design or very complicated. They can deal with a great number of subjects of which a few are Tibetan theology, astrology, pharmacology, lives of Buddhas, saints and deities, and mandalas.

Mandalas

Mandalas are graphic, geometric representations of the cosmos — "psychocosmograms" symbolising the order and harmony achieved by a truly enlightened mind. They have great power, being seen as concentrated areas where the forces of the universe are gathered. ("Manda" means "essence", while "La" means "container".)

The design is symmetrical, based on circles and squares, with a central focal point. In Tantric Buddhism, where the mandala is used to support meditation, adepts seek to absorb its power. Sometimes a mandala takes the form of an elaborate, four-gated city — a "palace of knowledge" — which the practitioner mentally enters and approaches the centre of in order to achieve a state of mystical unity with the Buddha.

Although not created primarily to please the eye, mandalas are often works of art with great stylistic elegance and beauty. They are most frequently displayed on thangkas but are also seen on the walls of temples and monasteries. A few monasteries, such as Sakya and Tashilhunpo, still create magnificent mandalas made of coloured sand.

Norbulingka, The Summer Palace (9-12, 3:30-6 Closed Sunday)

Norbulingka, meaning Jewel Park, now renamed People's Park, lies 3 km.
(2 miles) west of the Potala, near the Lhasa Hotel. Palaces, pavilions, a zoo,
gardens and woods cover 40 hectares (100 acres). It has the finest trees in
Lhasa and its air of deliberate light-heartedness makes it less demanding than
most sights in the city.

The Seventh Dalai Lama put up the first summer palace in 1755 and
each successive ruler added his own buildings. The current Dalai Lama built a
new palace in the 1950s shortly before he left Tibet. Although considerably
damaged, Norbulingka is now undergoing complete restoration.

One of Lhasa's greatest annual pageants used to be the Dalai Lama's
springtime move from his winter to his summer palace. In a magnificent
procession of lamas, nobles in the costumes of their rank, soldiers, musicians
on horseback and banners, the God-King was borne along in a gilded,
curtained palanquin while monks carried his belongings wrapped up in yellow
silk. The Dalai Lama, his family and high dignitaries entered inner walled
gardens containing the palaces, while teachers, servants and bodyguards
occupied surrounding buildings. During the summer, nobles were invited to
watch operas and other open-air performances.

The elaborate gate of entry, guarded by comical white lions and huge
red doors, was built by the Thirteenth Dalai Lama in this century. A road
followed to the right leads past ragged lawns to the **New Summer Palace**
which stands inside a spacious, walled garden. Its traditional Tibetan
architecture is modified by large windows and a double-storey entrance with
painted eaves in Ming Dynasty style.

Visitors can enter for Rmb. 2, after removing their shoes, and are
conducted in groups by a palace guide. The rooms on view upstairs include a
main throne hall above the entrance, the Dalai Lama's private apartment, an
audience hall and his mother's apartment.

The style throughout is a bizarre mixture of religious-traditional and
modern. The main throne hall is bright and airy with a statue of young
Sakyamuni occupying the higher of the two thrones. Opposite, a superb
mural tells Tibet's mythical early history from its founding by the holy monkey
through Songtsen Gampo's building of the Jokhang. The adjacent wall
recounts the founding of Samye Monastery by King Trisong Detsen.

The palace remains exactly as the Dalai Lama left it in 1959. His own
apartment juxtaposes carved Tibetan cabinets with heavy, Art-Nouveau
armchairs hauled over the Himalayas on porters' backs. Sacred images look
down on an antique Russian radio and a Philips console still containing his
old 78 rpm records. One amusing detail in the Audience Hall is often
overlooked: on the left-hand wall when facing the throne, near the back
corner, is a mural like a photo-montage showing the Dalai Lama's family and

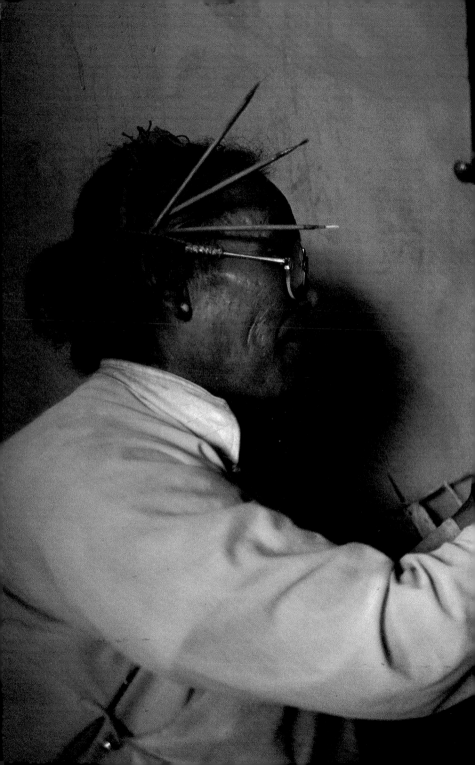

an international delegation of diplomats in among gods and demons.

The Artificial Lake, usually dry, and the Thirteenth Dalai Lama's little temple are in a walled compound adjoining the New Summer Palace's garden. Two pavilions with charming, carefree murals stand on a small island. On the east side, through another wall, an inner, unkempt garden backs up to the Old Summer Palace and holds small buildings formerly used for studying, meeting and living , still unrepaired. The 18th-century **Old Summer Palace** is reached from the road outside. Its dark, low-ceilinged, elaborate rooms are being restored and some of its stolen treasures have been returned, but at present only the handsome courtyard is open.

To the west is a small, fairly well-kept **zoo** with a collection of Tibetan animals such as snow lynx, white-bibbed Himalayan bears, fanged deer (*lageh*) and red, ring-tailed lesser pandas.

Not to be missed is the farthest temple group called the **Kasang**. The main temple contains one of the finest collections of thangkas anywhere. Entry costs Rmb. 2. Bring a flashlight. Some 70 hanging thangkas depict mandalas, Buddha life series, a herbal pharmacopoeia, a bestiary, etc. — a magnificent array. One wall displays 48 jewelled, brocaded Bodhisattvas and Taras in glass cases, and the Dalai Lama's throne. Just west of the main temple, the small Deki hall with steep steps has delightful murals.

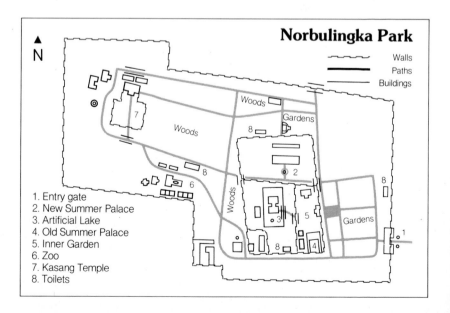

Norbulingka Park

N

- - - - Walls
——— Paths
——— Buildings

Woods
Gardens
Woods
Woods
Gardens

1. Entry gate
2. New Summer Palace
3. Artificial Lake
4. Old Summer Palace
5. Inner Garden
6. Zoo
7. Kasang Temple
8. Toilets

Monasteries and Monks

For 1,000 years Tibet was run by its monasteries or *gompas* that overlooked every town and settlement. A handful were great monastic cities, like Drepung and Sera, with thousands of monks. Several score, like Samye, housed about 500. Most were small, without land holdings, supported by the monks' relatives. Monasteries were the pillars of Tibet.

Under the rule of the Dalai Lamas, monasteries were free from taxation and they formed independent economic units. If they owned land, they held the local people as serfs. Trade and commerce were an integral part of their existence. The bigger ones accumulated vast wealth.

Every family in Tibet was expected to give at least one son to the monkhood. It is estimated that about one fifth of Tibet's male population was made up of celibate monks. The religious life, open to all, was the only avenue to education, a rise in social status or power. A monk brought honour and merit to his family and might, after long study, become a lama. The monasteries were the only centres of learning, art, literature, or medicine in Tibet. They embodied every formal aspect of the culture.

The structure of authority throughout Tibet depended on "incarnate lamas" — monks, discovered as small children, who were thought to be the reincarnations of previous abbots or lamas and not infrequently found in the families of powerful nobles. About 4,000 of these *tulkus* existed at any one time. At the pinnacle stood the Dalai and Panchen Lamas who were claimed as incarnations of a Bodhisattva and a Buddha. Tibet was governed by the Dalai Lama, along with his Regent, Cabinet, and a Council made up of the abbots of principal monasteries and lay noblemen, who owned much of Tibet's land and were rich and influential in their own right.

Boys generally became monks at the age of seven; girls — many fewer — became nuns at ten. Only the brightest entered a scholarly life within the monastery schools. Many more became clerks, craftsmen, builders, artists, cooks, housekeepers or "monk soldiers" who were feared for their ferocity.

Those who became educated followed a long course of study, examinations and initiations that lasted for 20-25 years. Examinations took the form of debates between the student monk and more learned lamas. Only after mastering logic, rhetoric, theology and close analysis of the Buddhist sutras could he become a lama himself. When he reached an advanced state of learning, he was considered eligible to follow the path of esoteric or occult doctrines and could develop paranormal powers.

Life for the monks, regardless of their status in the monastery, was rigorous. They rose before dawn and were occupied all day with religious services, administrative tasks, study, vigils, sutra-chanting, recitation, memory work, and the never-ending chores of communal life.

Common Tibetan Symbols

Some symbols recur on the walls of almost every temple, shrine and monastery, or on the walls of private houses. The most common decorative motifs of all are the Eight Sacred Emblems of Buddhism, as follows:

Dharma Wheel *(chakra)* — represents the unity of all things and symbolises Sakyamuni himself.

Conch Shell *(dun)* — used in Buddhist worship as a trumpet or offertory vessel and symbolises the "spoken word".

Lotus Flower *(padma)* — as the flower rises from muddy roots, so Nirvana arises from this shabby world and thus it symbolises purity.

Umbrella *(gdugs)* — is a token of royalty and symbolises the protection of the Dharma (Faith).

Golden Fish *(gser-na)* — as water allows fish to swim freely, so Buddhist belief emancipates the soul. They symbolise spiritual liberation.

Vase *(bum-pa)* — is used as a storage urn or a sacred receptacle and thus symbolises hidden treasures.

Banner of Victory *(dpal-be)* — a unique Buddhist object, the cylindrical layered banner symbolises victory over ignorance and death.

Endless Knot *(apal-be)* — an auspicious geometric diagram, it symbolises the unity of all things and the illusory character of time.

Some other common symbols are the following:

Wheel of Life — Found in vestibule murals. The hub shows the "three poisons": greed, hate and delusion (pig, snake, cock). The six big sections show all realms of existence: Heaven (top); Demi-gods (top left); Humankind (top right); Hell in awful detail (bottom); Hungry Ghosts with big bellies but tiny necks (low right); Animals (low left). The demon of Impermanence holds the whole wheel.

Mystical Seal of the Kalicakra — Usually among vestibule murals. It symbolises the highest of all initiations into occult knowledge, which can only be performed by a Dalai Lama.

Swastika — Found in mosaic floors or painted on homes. Ancient symbol. In Tibet it means good fortune. Strict followers of Buddhism draw it clockwise, followers of Bon anticlockwise.

Allegory of Cooperation — Found among murals. Bird brings a seed from afar and plants it. Rabbit manures the tree while eating grass under it. Monkey waters it while eating sweet fruit. Elephant comes to enjoy its shade and protect it. Thus was the Earth prepared for mankind.

Wind Horse *(lung-ta)* — Printed on prayer flags. Symbol of good luck with Three Jewels of Buddhism on his back. He takes prayers to Heaven by wind.

Sun and Moon — Painted on village houses. Ancient archetypal symbol for the source of light, union of opposites. In Tibet it is a folk sign for good luck and protection against evil spirits

Drepung Monastery (Admission Rmb.3.)

Drepung lies 8 km. (5 miles) west of Lhasa on a main road, then 3 km.(1¾ miles) north on a steep, unpaved road. Its name means "Rice Heap", after its jumble of white buildings piled up against Mount Gyengbuwudze.

Drepung was the biggest and richest monastery in Tibet. Its lamas, who helped to train each young Dalai Lama, could guess how a new God-King would rule — as a leader or as a tool of the Regent. Drepung housed the Nechung, the State Oracle. In a bizarre ceremony, the Oracle, in a trance, would utter prophecies on which the rulers based vital decisions.

Drepung was founded in 1416 by a disciple of Tsong Khapa, with a noble family as patron. The Fifth Dalai Lama enlarged it and ruled there while the Potala was being built. At its height Drepung had over 10,000 monks. It governed 700 subsidiary monasteries and owned vast estates.

In 1959, 6,000 monks lived there. Half, including all the high lamas, fled with the Dalai Lama. The rest went home, took up trades and married. A handful of elderly monks stayed on at the monastery, labouring on a 20-hectare (50 acre) farm that the Chinese let them keep. Today, about 400 monks and novices live there, and their orchards make them a profit.

The monastery was divided into four "Tantric colleges" which, at the highest level, specialised in different branches of knowledge. Each had its own chanting hall, dormitories, kitchens and offices. The entire monastic community assembled only for special ceremonies and festivals.

The chanting halls are all built on a similar plan, facing south with a courtyard in front. A big vestibule, with stairs to the roof at its east end, has big murals that typically include the Four Heavenly Kings (p.59) and the Wheel of Life (p.79). These are worth a good look. The chanting hall, hung with *thangkas* and "victory banners" (p.78), has closely spaced pillars with rows of cushions between, each holding a monk's robe and cap. Murals decorate the walls. Stairs on the left go to the roof. The north wall is a long altar. Behind it are elaborate chapels. The chanting hall should be walked through in a clockwise direction. It is often dark so bring a flashlight. The roof contains a hollow pavilion whose windows illuminate the chanting hall beneath. It is surrounded by a painted gallery. Higher roof levels hold chapels. The top level, supporting the golden finials, has a splendid view.

Approaching Drepung, you see the **Nechung Temple** on the right. This was the Oracle's home. The temple is in bad repair and its outer buildings are used as a farm. Higher, outside Drepung proper, are a shop, food stalls and a parking space. Stone steps lead up to the monastery city.

A lane running up the centre leads first to the **Nuosenle** college's chanting hall. Splendid murals on its south wall show a finely detailed Chenrezi in a circle of hands and eyes (left) and Yamantaka (p.59) with the Eight Guardians (right). Gold stupas on the altar and in the chapel are tombs of the Second, Third and Fourth Dalai Lamas. Butter and *tsampa* sculptures (p.90) fill a glass case on the altar. The Chapel behind has fine drawings on its plain red walls and in a glass case is a doll-sized Oracle in full regalia, with crown and armour, prophesying with open mouth. The Oracle appears in various forms all through the monastery.

If chanting is going on, the monks do not mind visitors going around the edge (clockwise). Discretion should be used in taking photographs. Drums and cymbals sometimes accompany the chanting. Periodically, a bell sends teenaged novices dashing out for jugs of butter tea to fill the wooden bowls of older monks. A kitchen just east of the chanting hall uses medieval stoves and gigantic churns, urns, cauldrons and implements.

Uphill to the west is the chanting hall of the **Tsug-gyeng** college. Instead of a vestibule, there is a small porch east of the entrance with a dais overlooking the courtyard. The dilapidated, half-empty interior is redeemed by a huge *thangka,* the old weapons tied onto pillars on the west side, and eight fine Bodhisattvas in the westernmost chapel. In addition, its roof houses Drepung's treasures. On the roof's west side, a chapel fronted by a covered porch contains its Holy of Holies, a giant gilded Buddha whose head and chest alone are visible. The cluttered chapel also holds a sacred conch shell with counter-clockwise whorls nearly hidden under white scarves. Pilgrims come here to prostrate. On the east is a chapel containing oracle dolls who are said to have spoken to special lamas in olden times, and Tsong Khapa's tooth in a gold reliquary.

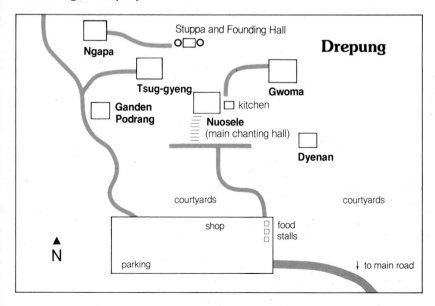

Behind this building is the carved rock face on which Drepung was founded. It now forms the wall of a little temple with white stupas on either side of it. The stick with which the founder beat his disciples is kept here in a silver scabbard by a lama who uses it to bless pilgrims, tapping them on their backs and shoulders with mock ferocity.

The small chanting hall of the **Ngapa** college nearby deserves a visit for the exquisite gold drawings on its red doors, portraying the history of the Dalai and Panchen Lamas. Straight down the hill from there is the **Ganden Podrang**, a three-tiered building from which the Fifth Dalai Lama reigned while the Potala was under construction. It should be entered from below to get its full effect. Steep steps lead up from its unimpressive front yard to an inner courtyard and a sudden, stunning view of its majestic façade.

Holy Mount Gyengbuwudze should attract hikers. A path from the west side of the monastery leads to the summit and involves a hard half-day's climb. On three occasions during summer Tibetans stream up it and spend the night singing, dancing and drinking *chang*.

Sera Monastery (Admission Rmb. 3.)

Sera lies on the northern edge of Lhasa at the base of Tatipu Hill. "Sera" means "Merciful Hail", denoting its rivalry with the "Rice Heap" (Drepung), since hail destroys rice. Sera was smaller than Drepung, with 7,000 monks, but was very rich and comparable in power. Today it has about 300 monks and some of its buildings house a farm.

Sera was founded in 1419 by one of Tsong Khapa's eight disciples. It became famous for its Tantric teachings while Drepung drew fame from its governing role. The monks of Sera were considered clever and dangerous. Its small army of warrior-monks, the *dob-dobs*, were admired as athletes but feared. Sera's rebelliousness sometimes posed a threat to the state. In 1947, its leaders planned to kill the Regent and install a rival. The plot failed, but witnesses recount that shops in Lhasa were barricaded and the nobles armed their servants for fear of rampaging monks.

A central lane and fairly simple layout make Sera easy to visit. Stalls by the main gateway sell soft drinks and snacks. A long driveway leads up to the monastery. Sera had three colleges like those at Drepung (p.82) but the chanting halls and chapels seem dark and more demonic.

Near the west side of the lane is the chanting hall of the **Gyetazang** college. Its holy west chapel contains an awesome, horse-headed demon-god, Ayaguriba, whose origins go back to the pre-Buddhist Bon religion. Behind this building is the **Debating Garden**. Novices can be seen preparing for monastic examinations by staging mock debates in the ritual way. Some sit cross-legged under the trees, while others run from group to group giving vigorous hand-claps to end a statement or make a point.

Masters and dignitaries sit on the raised tiers when a real examination takes place.

Sera's rock paintings are on the east mountainside. Notable are a blue Yamantaka with Prajina (p.59), Tsong Khapa above and Sera's first abbot, Sakya Yeshe, at the top. From here you can enter **Tsug-gyeng** college's chanting hall at roof level and, in an east chapel, find Sera's greatest treasure — a gilded Chenrezi with hundreds of hands and eyes. A colossal Maitreya can be seen from both the roof and the chanting hall.

Across the lane, the **Ngawa** chanting hall has many interesting objects but the **Drezame** college's chanting hall down the hill is truly remarkable. It has the best vestibule murals anywhere, especially its Wheel of Life.

One kilometre (¾ mile) east of Sera is an isolated rock where "sky burials" take place at dawn. Since frozen ground prevents normal burial and scarce fuel prohibits cremation, Tibetans learned to break the bodies of their dead into small pieces and feed them to the birds. Vultures, ravens and kites swoop down when the body-breakers, called *domdens*, have done their work. The whole gruesome process takes about two hours. Tourists are unwelcome. Go at your own risk!

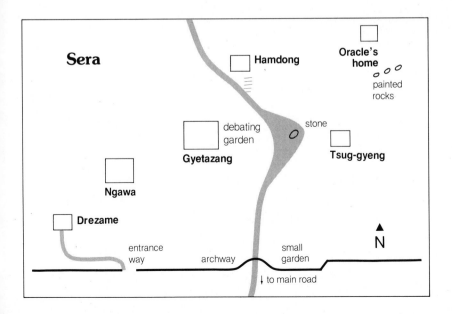

Common Religious Objects

Throughout Tibet, monks and
laymen have always used religious
articles as part of their daily lives.
Some of those most commonly
encountered are listed below:

Prayer Flag — Found in clusters
fluttering on roofs, mountain passes,
strung across rivers, above paths, etc.
Prayers and mantras printed by
woodblock on five colours of cotton
cloth are thought to be carried
heavenward by the wind.

Prayer Wheel — A hollow cylinder
containing printed prayers or sutras.
Every rotation equals a recitation of
the contents. In all sizes, most are
hand-held or hand-turned in fixed
rows around temples. Some are
turned by water or heat.

Dorje and Bell — The *dorje*
represents a thunderbolt,
fundamental symbol of Tantric faith.
It is used with the bell in all rituals.
The note of the bell, or *trilpu*, is said
to drive away evil by its magic music.

Mani Stone — A smooth stone
inscribed with the universal mantra
Om Mani Padme Hum. Found in
piles near temples and beside pilgrim
paths.

Juniper Hearth — Big stupa-
shaped fireplace found near temples
and holy spots, fuelled with juniper
wood whose sacred, fragrant smoke
constitutes an offering and bestows
blessing.

Butter and Tsampa Sculpture —
Torma or "holy food", ritually
presented to the gods, is usually a
cone of coloured tsampa (barley
meal) supporting decorated
medallions of butter. Elaborate,
gilded versions made at New Year
remain on altars in glass cases
throughout the year.

Chokpori Hill

Chokpori, the Medicine King Hill, is one of Central Tibet's four holy mountains, (none of them very high) and the only one near Lhasa. Holy mountains, because of their sacred nature, were considered to be the soul of the country. They preserved and protected the pilgrims who visited them. Today, Chokpori is topped by a tall, steel antenna.

Legend tells that the first doctor and founder of Tibetan medicine, named Yudo Gampo, made his home on Chokpori during the reign of King Songtsen Gampo. At the same period, one of the king's Tibetan wives made a temple in a cave on the east side of the hill. Much later, in the 17th century, the Fifth Dalai Lama established a monastic medical college on its summit which remained the chief one in Tibet for 300 years. It was bombarded by artillery during the uprising of 1959 and the ruins were removed in 1983 to make way for the antenna.

The middle slopes are encircled by a pilgrim footpath. Prayer flags, rock paintings, small shrines, piles of mani stones and juniper fires punctuate the route. A small crater is worn into the limestone cliff where devotees have scratched away powder to place on their tongues, believing in the medicinal properties of the mountain itself.

Palalubu Temple

This small, ancient cave-temple just off the main road in front of the Potala should not be missed. A lane, festooned with prayer flags, turns south at the foot of Chokpori Hill, opposite the spot where the rocky outcropping at the west end of the Potala meets the road. (This used to be the site of Lhasa's massive West Gate.) The white temple is built into the hillside above the lane, 100 m. (300 ft.) along it.

Palalubu was one of five temples built by King Songtsen Gampo's wives. The Jokhang, popularly attributed to Wen Cheng, the Chinese princess, was more probably founded by his Nepalese wife, Princess Tritsun. Ramoche (see below) was Wen Cheng's temple. His first Tibetan wife chose the caves on Medicine King Hill as the site for hers. The other two Tibetan wives founded a shrine named Pabunka above the present site of Sera Monastery and a temple 20 km. (12 miles) south of Lhasa.

Palalubu Temple, ascending the face of a cliff, is hardly more than a façade enclosing the cave within. Other buildings cluster in steps around it, housing a little community of monks. The gateway, at street level, leads into a courtyard where a deep cave has recently been refurbished to include numerous images set in glassed niches. Steep steps lead up to a hospitable antechamber a few steps below the original cave. This room serves as the monks' all-purpose room for chanting, doing household tasks and making large *tsampa* and butter sculptures (p.90). The cave itself is hollowed out around a central rock column with stone Buddha statues carved into its four sides. The walls display a frieze of relief sculptures, including one contemporary figure of Songtsen Gampo. Small and friendly, ancient Palalubu Temple has more charm than many of Lhasa's grander sites.

Lingkhor

The Lingkhor was Lhasa's circular, outer pilgrim road, matching its inner twin, the Barkhor (p.38). The Lingkhor was 8 km. (5 miles) long, enclosing Old Lhasa, the Potala and Chokpori. In former times it was crowded with men and women covering its length in prostrations, beggars, and pilgrims approaching the holy city for the first time. The road passed through willow-shaded parks where Tibetans loved to picnic in summer and watch open-air operas on festival days. New Lhasa obliterated most of the Lingkhor, but one stretch remains west of Chokpori. A bridge about 1 km. (¾ mile) west of the Potala on the main road, with green buildings beyond it on the right, is the landmark. The Lingkhor goes left before the bridge between walls and willow trees. After making a turn to the right at a small stream, it peters out at a duck pond. Open-air Tibetan operas are still performed within earshot of this pond on high festival days, one of which often falls in June (p.184).

Ramoche Temple

Often erroneously referred to as "Little Jokhang", Ramoche stands among small lanes in the north part of Old Lhasa. It originally housed Wen Cheng's statue of Sakyamuni, now the Holy of Holies of the Jokhang. In the 8th or 9th century, nobody knows why, an exchange was made and the Nepalese princess's small bronze statue of Sakyamuni aged eight was enshrined at Ramoche instead.

The temple was gutted and partially destroyed in the 1960s and the bronze statue disappeared. Many years later half of it was found in a rubbish pit in Lhasa, the other half was found marked as scrap-metal in Peking. Now repaired and temporarily housed in the Jokhang, it will be returned to Ramoche and the care of its 30 monks when restoration of the building is completed. The roof of the temple gives a fine view over Old Lhasa and down into the courtyards where Tibetans live.

Mosque and Moslem Quarter

Many people are surprised to learn of Lhasa's substantial Moslem community. Moslems from Ladakh were known in Tibet from early times as traders. When the Fifth Dalai Lama took Ladakh into his religious sphere of influence

in the 17th century, a small community of Moslems flourished in Lhasa, many of them working as butchers. Later, they were eclipsed by immigrants from Moslem areas north of Tibet. Today, Lhasa's Moslem quarter lying southeast of the Barkhor in Old Lhasa comprises about 1,000 families. The mosque of mixed Tibetan and Islamic architecture is its focal point for Friday prayers and Moslem holidays. Several nearby restaurants serve halal food (p.43).

Tibetan Traditional Hospital (Admission for guided tour Rmb. 10)

The Hospital, which includes Mendzekhang Medical College, is located on the north side of Renmin Lu, one block west of the Jokhang Temple. It gives interesting insights into the ancient art of Tibetan medicine.

Throughout history, few Tibetans have benefited from medical care, relying instead on charms, amulets and common sense. Their lack of hygiene, still all too evident, belies the existence of a profound and complicated medical tradition.

Tibetan medical theory evolved from several sources. King Songtsen Gampo was treated by the famous "Galen of Persia", who was invited to Tibet by his wife, Wen Cheng. Chinese and Indian physicians were also present at his court, and the Tibetan "Medicine King", Yudo Gampo, exerted his influence from Chokpori Hill. The appearance of numerous "Medicine Buddha" images in the 10th century points to a close connection with Indian medical theory and practice.

Knowledge of anatomy came from Chinese texts and diagrams and from Tibetan *domdens*, the body-breakers who dissected corpses for "sky burial" (p.87). Complex surgery, including that of the heart and brain, is known to have been carried out up to the 9th century, when the king banned surgery for evermore after his mother died during an operation.

Tibet's first medical school was set up by King Trisong Detsen (p. 50) in the 8th century. The second one was the renowned Chokpori school established by the Fifth Dalai Lama in the 17th century. Even with several smaller monastic schools in operation, a need for more doctors prompted the modern-minded Thirteenth Dalai Lama to found a third major school, Mendzekhang Medical College, in 1916.

Tibetan medical theory, based on 8th-century Tantric texts, required at least 11 years of training for future doctors. By committing thousands of pages to memory, a student became familiar with a fundamental theory of "humours", not unlike those known to medieval Europeans: "wind" moving within the skeleton, "bile" in the blood, and "phlegm" in the flesh, fat and fluids. Good health resulted from a stable balance between all three, which could not have been easy to achieve considering that the Tantras enumerated 84,000 different illnesses.

After grasping the theory, a student visualised a huge, schematic "Tree of Medicine", whose roots, trunks, twigs and leaves represented all branches of medicine from embryology to pharmacology. Months were spent in wild areas collecting and identifying the herbs that went into the making of some 2,000 drug preparations. Animal and mineral products, like ground tiger's tooth and pearls, also went into medicines. (It has been said that at one time the most prized pill of all included the mixed excrements of the Dalai and Panchen Lamas.)

Finally, the student doctor encountered patients and learned the vital tool of Tibetan medicine, "pulse diagnosis". A doctor had to develop such sensitivity that each of six fingers had two distinct points from which to monitor a patient's pulse and gather information about all the internal organs. Certain pulses were described by weird comparisons, like "a vulture attacking a bird, who stops, plunges, beats his wings quickly, stops again and resumes flight" or, of a moribund patient, "the saliva of a drooling cow, moving in the wind"! Acupuncture, moxibustion and blood-letting were additional areas of study.

Today, the students at Mendzekhang Medical College complete the core of their studies in four years and half of them are now women, but many aspects of their training remain unchanged. Surgery is still not a part of it. (This is handled in Lhasa by the four top Chinese hospitals.) In 1986 the college will be upgraded to a medical university with its own campus. The hospital expanded into its present building in 1978. It has only 25 beds, which are used for emergencies, but it routinely handles 600-700 outpatients a day. The top floor houses a library containing the Medical Tantras wrapped in silk and magnificent teaching *thangkas* (p.70). Anatomical charts mounted on brocade are over 300 years old. Finely detailed drawings in colour depict medicinal plants and the animal and mineral sources of medicine. An ancient view of embryology is remarkably accurate by modern standards. A senior physician may be observed taking a patient's pulse with deep concentration. Across the hall is the arcane Astrological-Astronomical Institute where research goes on into astrological diagnosis. Star maps, charts and compilations of symbols fill the walls. Doctors pore over the sutras and diagrams of the heavens, making calculations on trays of sand. They not only work out astrological signs for years ahead but also predict the weather.

The two lower floors are given over to small clinics. Some of them administer purely traditional medicine, including herbal treatment, acupuncture and moxibustion. Others have relatively modern equipment like electrocardiographs and X-ray machines. Patients can choose the type of clinic they prefer. The whole place is redolent with the smell of, not disinfectant as one might expect in a hospital, but yak butter.

The central lobby of the hospital is filled with Tibetans waiting with fistfuls of prescriptions outside a vast pharmacy-cum-dispensary. Be sure to arrange a visit inside it. Here are hundreds of orderly drawers, hand-decorated cabinets, vats, tubs and mountains of herbs, seeds, roots, pills, tablets and elixirs. Twenty-two pharmacists, grinders and mixers make up the medicines that are dispensed through small windows to the lines of patients waiting outside in the lobby.

Lhasa Carpet Factory

The factory is located just south of Yanhe Dong Lu, near Tibet University. It produces traditional Tibetan rugs that are exported worldwide through Canton. Although the actual weaving and finishing are done by hand, using old-style vertical looms, some stages of the process, such as spinning, are now mechanised and the dyeing is not done in the factory. This factory is more modern than either the one in Gyantse (p.122) or in Nedong (p.148). It is the biggest rug factory in Tibet, employing 180 workers. Traditionally, Tibetan women are the weavers and men the spinners, but both work on rugs today.

The rugs are typically quite small, with bold designs, bright colours and a deep, even pile — about 60 knots per square inch. Rug weaving is an ancient craft in Tibet but because it was not for sacred purposes it was never considered an art. As a result, there are no rugs verifiable earlier than the 19th century. Chemical dyes first appeared in Central Asia around 1870 and are now very widely used. The use of durable cotton warps and wefts was introduced into Tibet in the early 20th century. A 2 X 1 m. (6 x 3 ft.) rug costs about Rmb. 400.

Tibetan Performing Arts School

This school, founded in 1980, moved to its present location opposite the Tibet Guesthouse in Lhasa's western suburbs in 1983. The school has about 90 students aged 12 to 20. The director, Mr. A Ke, is a well-known Tibetan dancer and choreographer. By arrangement, visitors can watch the students practising Tibetan dances in the studio. Some will become members of cultural groups performing throughout Tibet and occasionally in China, perhaps even abroad. Others will join the Tibetan opera, while some will remain at the school as teachers. It is also possible to visit the music studios where various instruments and singing are taught. A group already performs with one of Lhasa's two opera companies. If they happen to be rehearsing in costume, there is a chance to get some exotic and colourful photographs.

Gumolingka Island

"Thieves' Park" is the literal translation of Gumolingka, a big island in the

Lhasa River close to the city. Legend says that petty criminals used to run from Lhasa and hide there. Today, though, it is a place of recreation for swimmers, lovers, drinkers and friends. It can be reached on foot by a narrow suspension bridge off Yanhe Xi Lu (Map, pp.36-37). The island changes size with the height of the river but there is always good swimming on the far side.

Droma Lakang Temple

This small temple is associated with Atisha's history-shaping visit to Tibet in the 11th century (p.50). It is located 27 km. (17 miles) south of Lhasa on the main road to Gonggar. The monks sometimes demand to see a permit from Lhasa to visit the temple; this can be obtained from CITS but a humbly offered donation of Rmb. 3-5 seems to be equally acceptable to the monks.

The temple, kept by four monks, is dedicated to the memory of Atisha, who stayed here, and his special deity, Tara. It consists of a vestibule with restored murals and a white stupa; a prayer wheel gallery around the main hall; and the hall itself which is divided into three chapels. The first two have richly adorned figures of goddesses and several copper stupas (p.121); Atisha himself is believed to have introduced these ubiquitous, domed towers to Tibet from India. The third chapel, dominated by giant statues, contains the stone throne from which Atisha preached to the people. A small statue of Atisha in a glass case now sits on the throne. Myth says that after Atisha taught the Tibetans, he crumbled a piece of stone in his hand, blew on the dust, and the giant figures took form. The three biggest are male Buddhas; all the others are Taras.

Ganden Monastery

The ruins of this great monastery lie about 70 km. (44 miles) east of Lhasa on a rough, unpaved road. A bus leaves from the Barkhor, by the juniper hearth behind the Jokhang, at 6.45 am. Trucks charge Rmb. 5 for the trip one way. The "Taxi Company" (p.42) charges Rmb. 100 for the round trip.

Situated at 4,300 m. (14,000 ft.) in a bowl like an amphitheatre, Ganden commands a dramatic view up and down the Lhasa River Valley. It was demolished by explosives in 1959 and further annihilated in the 1960s.

Ganden was Lhasa's second biggest monastery and at times the strongest of the great three in dominating the government administration. Tsong Khapa established it in 1409, earlier than either Drepung or Sera, as a place to train moral, disciplined monks and to work out the reformed version of Tibetan Buddhism that soon evolved into the Yellow Hat Sect (p.51). Today, Ganden is being rebuilt, largely by local, volunteer effort. About 200 monks have returned, without permission from the official Bureau of Religious Affairs. Two main chanting halls and several other buildings have been reconstructed and are in daily use.

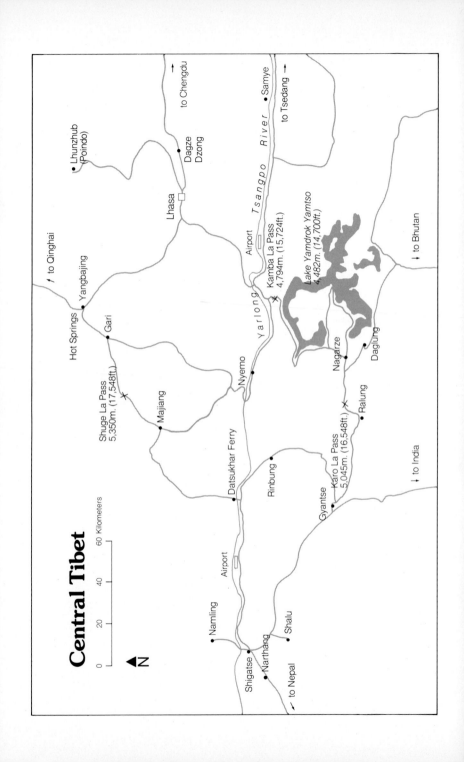

Shigatse

Shigatse, population 40,000, is Tibet's second largest city, with an altitude of 3,900 m. (12,800 ft.). It is the administrative centre of a vast area, formerly called Tsang, that includes most of West-Central Tibet. Historically, it often rivalled Lhasa, which controlled U, or East-Central Tibet. The two regions are still referred to as Front Tibet (Lhasa's area), and Back Tibet (Shigatse's area).

Shigatse stands near the confluence of the Yarlong Tsangpo and Nyangchu (Liancuo) Rivers. The latter flows from southeast to northwest, watering a broad, beautiful valley 100 km. (62 miles) long, with Gyantse at one end and Shigatse at the other. It is one of Tibet's richest farming areas. Barley, rape seed, wheat, beans and many varieties of vegetables colour the valley with all shades of green in summer, and with bright yellow patches in June and July, when the rape flower is in bloom.

Shigatse was previously both a stronghold and a monastery city. Today, as with all sizeable Tibetan towns, an undistinguished, modern, Chinese section equals the old town in size. Shigatse forms a horseshoe around a rocky prominence that was formerly topped by an awesome fortress. At the western tip, beneath Mount Dromari, lies Tashilhunpo Monastery, seat of the Panchen Lamas (p.110) and one of Tibet's four greatest monasteries.

Getting There

Southern Route One road from Lhasa to Shigatse follows the old caravan trade route to India as far as Gyantse, then turns northwest along the Nyangchu River. It crosses two high passes. The distance is about 300 km. (188 miles); the trip usually takes six hours. Once past the Yarlong Tsangpo bridge, the road is unpaved.

The first pass, 82 km. (51 miles) from Lhasa, is the Kamba La, 4,794 m. (15,724 ft.) high. This is the traditional boundary between Front and Back Tibet. The views are dramatic. North, down a long, barren valley, glistens the Yarlong Tsangpo River. To the south lies a finger of the oddly scorpion-shaped Yamdrok Yamtso, Tibet's third largest lake. In sunshine it shines sapphire-blue, with bright green triangles of farmland on its shores under looming, treeless peaks. The second pass, 163 km. (101 miles) from Lhasa, is the Karo La, altitude 5,045 m. (16,548 ft.). It offers no sudden views and can only be noticed by its stone cairn and clusters of prayer flags. Just beyond, on the right, a glacier approaches the road but a half-hour scramble is needed to reach it. Other glaciers dot the mountaintops on both sides. Following the upper Nyangchu River through rocky hills, the road emerges in a narrow valley with mud-brick telephone poles marching along it like little fat men. At Gyantse, the landscape opens into a fertile plain that leads straight to Shigatse.

Northern Route An alternative, less-travelled route loops west from
Lhasa along the edge of the great northern plateau. The distance is 340 km.
(210 miles) and takes about seven hours. An unpaved road branching west
from Yangbajing (p.151), 87km. (54 miles) from Lhasa, crosses three high
passes. First, the Shuge La, 5,350 m. (17,548 ft.), gives a view of snow-
capped mountains and grazing yak herds. The next two, the Dunggu La,
4,960 m. (16,268 ft.), and the Gangdisi La, 4,100 m. (13,448 ft.), would be
easy to miss except for piles of stones and prayer flags as the road descends
through wild valleys, known mainly to nomads, towards the Yarlong
Tsangpo River. A tug-drawn barge ferries vehicles across at Datsukhar. The
road follows the south bank upstream to Shigatse. Ideally, visitors should take
the southern Gyantse route one way between Lhasa and Shigatse, as well as
the northern route, to see two quite different faces of Tibet.

Hotels

日喀则饭店
Shigatse Hotel (Rikaze Fandian) This new, 250-bed hotel affects a
"neo-monastery" style. By local standards it is above average, but in fact its
services are awful. Rooms have private bathrooms with dubious plumbing.
Budget travellers can struggle to get into a dormitory. CITS, with offices here,
is hard pressed to provide services. It has only a limited number of guides,
who are mostly inexperienced, and extra vehicles are few. Price about Rmb.
80 per bed per day, including three meals; Rmb. 6.50 per bed (dormitory)
per day, excluding meals.

日喀则第二招待所
Shigatse No. 2 Guesthouse (Rikaze Di Er Zhaodaisuo) This complex of
one-storey buildings has rooms with a wide range of prices. There is no
plumbing but hot and cold water for washing is provided. A main dining
room offers good, ample, Chinese food and beer. A small kitchen annex can
give cheaper food to guests bringing their own bowls. Prices between Rmb. 5
and 60 per bed per day.

日喀则第一招待所
Shigatse No. 1 Guesthouse (Rikaze Di Yi Zhaodaisuo) Located across the
street just west of Tashilhunpo's main gate, this typical truck-stop inn offers
friendly, simple accommodation to travellers. About 25 rooms, with three
beds each, are built on two levels around a large court, like a caravanserai. A
small shack in the yard has hot water and a tap with cold, for washing. A
kitchen run by the Tibetan staff cooks plain, cheap Chinese-style meals on
request for visitors. Price Rmb. 5 per bed per day. There is a possibility that
this guesthouse, like other truck-stop inns, may be put off limits to foreigners.

Sights

Background Shigatse, capital of Tsang, took part for centuries in struggles to control Tibet — rivalries between the regions of U (Lhasa) and Tsang, and between the reformed Yellow Hat and old Red Hat sects. Tibet had stagnated for 200 years after its last king, Lang Darma, (p.50) tried to stamp out religion. Then, in 1042, Atisha arrived from India and his Tibetan disciples set off a surge of intellectual and religious activity. Old monasteries were revived and hundreds of new ones started in all the settled areas. Battles for power were soon raging because Tibet still had no central government to control them.

In Tsang, Buddhist monks and priests of the old Bon religion attacked each other with words and sorcery. The three big noble families of the region joined the fray. These lords, with huge wealth in land holdings, claimed divine ancestry like the former kings. They now founded important monasteries such as Sakya (p.160) and Shalu (p.115). They made sure that members of their families became monks and abbots, then began jockeying for wider control by making foreign alliances, notably with the Mongols. In 1206, Genghis Khan's hordes threatened Central Tibet. Without a fight, Tibet's nobles offered submission and certain monasteries profited from getting a foreign patron, especially Sakya, in the centre of Tsang, which received both gifts and an invitation to send Buddhist missionaries to Mongolia. Kublai Khan, the future Emperor of China, chose Sakya's abbot to be his tutor in 1254 and as a reward gave Sakya sovereignty over all Tibet. There was much friction and strife under Sakya's rule. Within a century Mongol power waned, Sakya declined and unstable infighting among sects and monasteries became the rule in Tibet once again.

In the 15th century, Tsong Khapa reformed Lamaism. His new Yellow Hat sect dominated U through the three great monasteries of Lhasa (Ganden, Drepung and Sera). But in spite of the establishment of a fourth important Yellow Hat monastery at Shigatse (Tashilhunpo), Tsang remained firmly in the hands of the Red Hats. In addition, the lords of Tsang became implacable enemies of the Yellow Hats and new wars erupted.

The Fifth Dalai Lama ended all this in the 17th century by doing what Sakya had done 400 years earlier: he got a mighty Mongolian patron. With a Mongol army he finally defeated Tsang and ended Red Hat hopes of power. From then on the Dalai Lama controlled all of Tibet and the Panchen Lama was to act as his spiritual right hand in Tsang.

Today, visitors to Shigatse can still see the different layers of history, from Yellow Hat Tashilhunpo Monastery back to Red Hat Shalu Monastery. And by looking carefully, counter-clockwise swastikas (p.79) can sometimes be observed on floors or walls — giving evidence that the ancient Bon religion has lived on to the present time.

The Panchen Lamas

The Panchen Lamas, abbots of Tashilhunpo Monastery, came into existence in the 17th century when the Fifth Dalai Lama gave this title to his beloved and learned tutor. "Panchen" means "Great Scholar". So-called "hidden texts" were then "discovered" that proved he was a reincarnation of Amitabha, the Buddha of Infinite Light, and traced the incarnations back two centuries to one of the first abbots of Tashilhunpo. He thus counted not as the first but as the Fourth Panchen Lama. In a similar fashion, the Great Fifth had already been established as an incarnation of Tibet's patron deity, Chenrezi, the Bodhisattva of Compassion. From the 17th century on, the Panchen and Dalai Lamas initiated one another as divine leaders and the older one served as tutor to the younger. When a Panchen Lama died, a search began at once for the infant boy who was believed to be his new incarnation, just like the Dalai Lamas (p.68).

Some Tibetans considered the Panchen Lamas even holier than the Dalai Lamas. By having no secular authority they were thought to be less tainted by worldly affairs. Foreigners named them "Tashi Lamas" (misappropriating the first syllables of Tashilhunpo) and created a myth that they were wise, all-knowing holy men. In fact, they mixed in politics, sometimes rivalled the Dalai Lamas and conducted independent foreign policies which foreign powers tried to exploit. There have been ten Panchen Lamas.

The First , Second and Third Panchen Lamas were all learned scholars and successive abbots of Tashilhunpo who upheld the Yellow Hat sect.

The Fourth (1569-1662) was the learned tutor of the Fifth Dalai Lama, who honoured him with divine status and the title of Panchen.

The Fifth (1663-1737) lived through the mixed-up succession to the Sixth Dalai Lama. In 1728 the Chinese emperor, hoping to divide Tibet, offered him sovereignty over all Western Tibet but he did not accept it.

The Sixth (1738-1780) was distinguished by his writings and interest in the world. He befriended George Bogle (p.46). The gold he naively sent as a gift to the Governor of India whetted Britain's interest in Tibet. He also travelled to China, but in Peking he caught smallpox and died.

The Seventh (1781-1854) was protected by China from Nepalese raids.

The Eighth (1854-1882) died before he got caught in foreign affairs.

The Ninth (1883-1937) had severe conflicts with the Thirteenth Dalai Lama. Both the Chinese and the British tried to woo him. Fearing revenge from the Dalai Lama for his support of China, he fled and died in exile.

The Tenth (b.1938) was born in China and not confirmed as a genuine incarnation until age 11. His close but stormy relations with Tibet's new Chinese administrators resulted in his virtual disappearance for many years after 1961. He now holds honorific positions and works in Peking. In the 1980s he returned twice to Tibet for short visits to Tashilhunpo.

Tashilhunpo Monastery (9-12 Admission Rmb. 2)

Tashilhunpo, meaning "Heap of Glory", was the seat of the Panchen Lamas. It lies at the foot of Dromari, or "Tara's Mountain", on the west side of Shigatse and is today one of Tibet's most active monasteries.

It was founded in 1447 by Tsong Khapa's youngest disciple, who was his nephew and the main organiser of the Yellow Hat sect. The early abbots, posthumously named the First, Second and Third Panchen Lamas, were learned scholars who often had to flee to the province of U from their fierce Red Hat opponents in Tsang.

The enlargement of Tashilhunpo took place mostly under the Fourth, Fifth and Sixth Panchen Lamas, after the Yellow Hat sect had been firmly established as Tibet's official religion. But it still had troubles. When the broad-minded Sixth Panchen Lama died of smallpox in Peking, his brother, the Treasurer of Tashilhunpo, stole his entire huge fortune. He refused to distribute it to the monastery or share it with his other brothers and he thereafter became the Governor of Tsang. Another brother, who lived in Nepal, led an army of Gurkha warriors to Shigatse in 1791, where they sacked and looted Tashilhunpo. The Chinese drove out the Nepalese and at the same time strengthened their influence over Tibet.

Tashilhunpo had over 4,000 monks and was organised like Lhasa's great monasteries. It had four Tantric "colleges", each with its own abbot. After the death of a Panchen Lama, these four abbots led the search for his infant

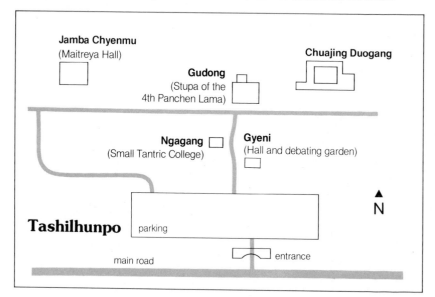

reincarnation, and one of them always acted as the prime minister of Tsang, under the control of the Dalai Lama in Lhasa.

Tashilhunpo was disbanded as a monastery by the Chinese army in 1960 while the Panchen Lama was absent. Less physical damage was inflicted than on many other sites and a handful of caretaker monks was allowed to remain. Today, there are 610 monks of whom 110 are young novices.

Layout The most remarkable object on the monastery grounds is an enormous Thangka Wall, nine storeys high, which stands like a huge drive-in movie screen, clearly visible from the city. This structure is used most of the year for storing three gigantic banners bearing images of the Buddha which are displayed on the wall for only three days a year during summer festivities.

The monastery itself, facing south, is one of the most spectacular in Tibet for the salmon-rose colour of its main buildings, set off by the ecclesiastical red-brown of the parapets and clear black-and-white trim. The buildings form a horizontal line: a gigantic Maitreya temple on the west, the Panchen Lama's palace (containing the stupa-tomb of the Fourth) in the middle, and on the east a cluster of buildings around a big courtyard that includes the main chanting hall, a sutra hall and chapels.

A path runs north from the main gate between white stone buildings and courtyards that house smaller chanting halls, the Debating Garden, dormitories and workshops. Pilgrims coming to Tashilhunpo bring bags of *tsampa* as offerings, rather than yak butter as in Lhasa.

The Maitreya Temple (Jamba Chyenmu), on the west side, is the tallest building of the monastery. It was erected in 1914 by the Ninth Panchen Lama to house a gigantic statue of the Maitreya Buddha, 26.2 m. (86 ft.) high. The statue sits on a splendid lotus throne in the "European" posture with its hands in the symbolic teaching pose. A single finger is 1.2 m. (almost 4 ft.) long. The statue contains 279 kg. (614 lb.) of gold and 150,000 kg. (330,000 lb.) of copper and brass, moulded on a wooden frame by Tibetan and Nepalese craftsmen. A clockwise walk around the back shows how this was done with metal sheets. Murals on either side of the door show a more active, antic style than any to be seen in Lhasa.

A lane leads east to the **Panchen Lama's Palace** (Gudong), entered by a door in its east side. Within, a narrow courtyard gives access to a temple containing the Fourth Panchen Lama's tomb. The temple vestibule has very large inscriptions at either end praising the Fourth Panchen Lama. Inside, the silver and gold stupa-tomb rivals any in the Potala for the splendour of its workmanship and jewels. Measuring 11 m. (36 ft.) in height, it contains 85 kg. (187 lb.) of gold and countless semi-precious stones. On the left is a statue in a wooden enclosure representing Amitabha, the Buddha of Infinite Light, whom the Panchen Lamas are thought to embody. An upper level has long chapels with embroidered silk *thangkas* that relate the lives and events surrounding all the Panchen Lamas. Most were made in Hangzhou, in the east of China, during the 1920s. Unfortunately, the living quarters of the Panchen Lama are no longer open to the public. The rooms are more modest and human than any in the Potala.

The flagstoned **Great Courtyard** (Chuajing Duogang), to the east, has walls covered by 1,000 repeated Sakyamunis, their hands in five symbolic poses (*mudras*). On the west side, the **Main Chanting Hall** contains the Panchen Lama's throne and two connected chapels. The left-hand one is devoted to an elaborately ensconced Sakyamuni with eight Bodhisattvas robed in brocade. The right-hand one is dedicated to Tara (p. 59), the goddess who sanctifies the mountain above, and whose image can be found throughout the monastery. A White Tara occupies the centre of the altar, with a Green Tara on either side.

The Gallery surrounding the courtyard leads to chapels on the east housing hundreds of tiny Buddha statues. Behind them, a **Sutra Hall** is the repository of some 10,000 hand-carved, wooden blocks used for printing the Buddhist scriptures. These are all Tibetan translations of the original Sanskrit. Tourists can buy coloured prayer flags and Tibetan lunar calendars which are printed here.

The Roof has several chapels. On the north side, above the chapels of the Chanting Hall, is the funerary stupa of the First Dalai Lama (Tsong Khapa's nephew, who founded Tashilhunpo), the only one not entombed in Lhasa. On the east side is a small "chamber of horrors" chapel. Painted demons, considered now to be defenders of Buddhism, betray their origins as the terrifying gods of the old animist Bon faith who only later were absorbed by Buddhism. On the south side is a charming Tara chapel.

Less frequently visited is the small chanting hall of the **Ngagang** college on the west side of the main north-south path, upstairs from a small courtyard. Here a morning chanting ceremony with musical instruments sometimes takes place. Pilgrims may circumambulate the hall, but tourists, especially photographers, should be sensitive to the religious atmosphere. Directly below the Panchen Lama's Palace, east of the main path, is the **Gyeni Chanting Hall** and the Debating Garden with many fine trees. The roof of the chanting hall has a bizarre chapel on the north side where two very tall guardians are formed from its structural columns by the use of masks and ancient armour. Outside it are some extraordinary animal murals that seem to have emerged from folklore and animism.

Pilgrim Walk

An interesting 3 km. (1¾ mile) walk leads back to the city by way of the giant Thangka Wall, the ruins of Shigatse's citadel or *dzong* and an open-air Tibetan market. It is important to do the walk returning from Tashilhunpo (not starting from Shigatse) so as to maintain a clockwise direction and avoid offending pilgrims on the path.

A sandy road parallel to the west wall of Tashilhunpo quickly becomes a well-worn path leading up behind the monastery, past prayer wheels and shrines, to the foot of the Thangka Wall which cannot, however, be entered. Many paths criss-cross Tara's Mountain above up to the sacred, flag-festooned peak. The path divides at the Thangka Wall, one branch descending beside the east wall to make a circle around the monastery, the other continuing level along the flank of the mountain towards Shigatse. After passing an array of carved and painted rocks it emerges below the rocky prominence that dominates the city. Here a hiker can either climb up to the ruins or take a right-hand route down to the market.

The *dzong* (fortress), totally destroyed in 1961, was once a small Potala covering the whole hilltop, with up-sweeping white walls that seemed to grow from the crags. It had a central Red Palace and turret-like fortifications at the outer ends. The formidable structure was seen as both a homage and a challenge to the power of Lhasa embodied in the real Potala. Only the foundations remain but the site gives a magnificent view over Shigatse and its surrounding valleys.

The Market below, just south of the *dzong*, consists of an organised street with neat, covered stalls where Tibetan artifacts, jewellery, cloth, leather, copperware, etc. are for sale. Visitors may find shopping here easier than on the Barkhor in Lhasa, and the variety is almost as good. Prices are all open to bargaining.

Shalu Monastery

This small monastery lies 22 km. (14 miles) south of Shigatse. For centuries it was renowned as a centre of scholarly learning and psychic training, and its mural paintings were considered to be the most ancient and beautiful in Tibet. Shalu still had 100 monks in this century and its reputation lasted up to its destruction in the 1960s. A small part of it, housing six monks, seven novices and a few superior murals, is still standing.

Shalu was founded in 1040 near a flourishing, long-vanished market town. It was the first of the major monasteries to be built by noble families of Tsang during Tibet's great revival of Buddhism. Shalu's monks kept in close touch with Sakya Monastery, founded soon afterwards, which was bigger and politically more powerful.

In 1329 an earthquake demolished Shalu. The Mongol Emperor of China ordered local lords to rebuild it in 1333. The new style was Mongolian: massive, inward-sloping walls around a main courtyard, strong woodwork and glazed roof tiles from Qinghai.

The man in charge of Shalu at the time of the earthquake was Buston (pronounced Budun), its 11th abbot. Buston (1290-1364) was enormously energetic. Not merely a capable administrator, he is still remembered as a prodigious scholar, writer and Tibet's most celebrated historian. He catalogued all of the Buddhist scriptures — 4,569 religious and philosophical works — and put them into a logical, usable order. He wrote countless commentaries of his own and produced new translations of many religious texts. In addition, he wrote a famous *History of Buddhism in India and Tibet* which scholars are still using today. Buston's activity naturally attracted other intellectuals to Shalu. Although the monastery was only intended to hold 500 monks, as many as 3,000 would assemble there for lectures.

After Buston's time, Shalu became an important centre of esoteric studies and psychic training. The avowed purpose of lamas who cultivated paranormal abilities was not to become magicians or miracle-workers but to attain philosophical enlightenment — a realisation, in the Buddhist tradition, that all earthly phenomena are mere creations of the mind. Nonetheless, after many years of training in intense concentration (often sealed up in caves in total darkness), the adepts are said to have performed extraordinary feats. The commonest, called *tumo*, was a monk's ability to raise his body temperature voluntarily to a level where he could live at frigid temperatures with only the lightest clothing. Long-distance runners called *lung-gom-pas* learned to cross Tibet's vast spaces with superhuman leaps while in a trance state, and served as messengers. Some masters were able to move their human consciousness into the bodies of birds, animals, or even dead people.

Illuminated monk

Others could become invisible at will by learning how to leave no impression upon the memories of people they encountered. Whether or not such feats actually took place with any regularity is impossible to say but most Tibetans firmly believe that they did.

The monastery stands in a small valley facing east. It is mostly destroyed; only the outer wall and the main building with damaged roofs are still standing, along with a few adjacent tumble-down structures.

The few remaining murals in good condition are in a chapel on the south side of the roof, which is reached by an exterior stone staircase.

Two charming 13th-century murals on the wall outside the chapel follow an iconographic scheme developed by Buston himself. To the right of the doorway is a primer of monastic discipline. At the top, Buston and two disciples are enveloped in clouds. Below, precise rules are laid out for the monks on what to wear, where to place their robes, when to bathe, how to behave under all circumstances. Eight monks demonstrate how they must sleep and meditate perched in trees when travelling away from the monastery. The mural on the left is an allegory in which an elephant, representing a human soul, evolves through many steps and earthly trials to Nirvana, becoming steadily whiter and purer as he progresses.

Inside are several intricate mandalas (p.70). Three exquisite examples are on the south wall behind the altar, each one 3 m. (10 ft.) in diameter and still in a good state of preservation. All the others, as well as the painted, coffered ceiling, have suffered various degrees of damage from forced neglect and rain entering through the roof. Mandalas were a speciality of Shalu. Formerly, the designs were also created out of coloured sand here, but these were never kept longer than a year.

The only other chapel open to visitors is on the west side of the roof. Remnants of former mandala murals are concealed by over 100 *thangkas*, most of which were embroidered in Hangzhou, eastern China, early in the 20th century. A fine *thangka* hanging over a small altar that stands alone was painted several decades ago by Shalu's present head monk. The large upper-storey porch over the wrecked chanting hall was the apartment of Buston and subsequent abbots but this cannot be visited. Money was allocated to Shalu Monastery in 1985 for repairs of the roofs and eventual restoration of some murals.

Narthang (Ladang) Monastery

The mud-brick ruins lie 15 km. (9 miles) west of Shigatse beside the main road. Founded in 1153 by one of Atisha's disciples, Narthang was the fourth great monastery of Tsang, with Shalu, Sakya and Tashilhunpo. Like Sakya, it was a big, square, walled compound in the Mongolian style. Parts of the high fortress walls are still standing.

Narthang was first famous for its scriptural teaching and monastic discipline. After the 14th century it gained great eminence as the oldest of Tibet's three great printing centres (the others being the Potala and Derge in eastern Tibet). The Fifth Panchen Lama took Narthang under the control of Tashilhunpo and it continued printing the Buddhist scriptures, the *Kanjur* and *Tenjur*, up until 1959. A few of the ancient woodblocks and early editions might have survived in the collection at Tashilhunpo.

Narthang's five main buildings and large chanting hall were razed to the ground in 1966. They had contained priceless 14th-century murals, probably painted by the artists of Shalu. Today, only the foundations can be discerned. One monk lives in a tiny dwelling at the centre of the site and works as a farmer.

The Summer Palace

The Panchen Lama's summer palace, built in 1950, lies one kilometre (3/4 mile) south of Tashilhunpo Monastery at the end of a straight road. It is not open to the public as the Panchen Lama still stays there on his occasional visits to Shigatse. A grand portal graces the high, enclosing wall on the east side. Around the back of the property the wall gives way to a fence from where two inner, walled compounds can be seen. The big yellow mansion is the residence. The white compound houses the kitchens, servants' quarters, etc. The grounds have some fine trees but are otherwise totally neglected. It is in no way comparable to the Norbulingka summer palace in Lhasa.

Shigatse Gold, Silver and Copper Crafts Factory

This primitive silver-working factory on the southern edge of Shigatse was set up in 1965. Ornamental cups, bowls, ewers and votive butter lamps are hand made by 17 master craftsmen and 49 workers, many of whom are young apprentices. They work primarily with hammers and small charcoal fires with bellows of hide. Gold and copperware vessels are also produced here, but no jewellery.

Coracle Ride

The traditional Tibetan boat for ferrying or fishing is an oval-shaped coracle made of willow branches and yak hide. It is virtually unsinkable and can be carried upstream on the back of one strong man. CITS plans to arrange short coracle trips for tourists on the Yarlong Tsangpo near Shigatse, through a beautiful stretch of the river known as the Dongga Valley.

Gyantse

Gyantse, altitude 3,800 m. (12,465 ft.), is about 210 km. (130 miles) from Lhasa and 95 km. (60 miles) from Shigatse. It was once Tibet's third most important city, lying at the head of the Nyangchu Valley astride the main routes from India and Nepal to Lhasa. In former times it was a fort, the centre of Tibet's wool trade and a gateway to the outside world. In recent years other places in Tibet have grown faster and in comparison it is now a fairly small town.

A high, rocky ridge topped by a ruined fortress runs through the middle of Gyantse, dividing it into two parts. On the west are a large monastery complex and part of the original city with a main market street. A newly built avenue leads around the outer edge right to the monastery. On the east is another section of the old town, including a rug factory and the principal approach to the citadel above. A few Chinese work units form a suburban ring around the Tibetan town.

There is a major crossroads at the southeast edge of Gyantse. Here the road from Lhasa runs straight ahead into the town and the right-hand turn leads into the suburbs. The left-hand road turning southwards leads a traveller either to Shigatse and Nepal or to Yadong and India.

Hotels

江孜镇第一招待所
Gyantse No.1 Guesthouse (Jiangzi Zhen Di Yi Zhaodaisuo) This is a typical truck-stop hotel, located about 250 m. (750 ft.) on the left beyond the big crossroads when reaching Gyantse from Lhasa. The main overnight rest stop in Gyantse, it has more than 50 beds in rooms around a central courtyard, similar to a caravanserai. There is a cold water tap in the courtyard and an attached kitchen with edible Chinese food. Truck drivers are the primary clients. At present there is no problem about foreigners staying here. Price ranges from Rmb. 2.50 to 4 per bed per day.

江孜县招待所
Gyantse County Guesthouse (Jiangzi Xian Zhaodaisuo) Just beyond the crossroads on the right, coming from Lhasa, this inn has approximately 15 rooms with three beds in each. It is a tolerable place with a cold water tap and a noodle shop outside the main gate. Price Rmb. 4 per bed per day.

Food is a problem in Gyantse — few eating houses, poor service and generally poor quality. Noodles are the principal fare. It is advisable to bring supplementary tinned food and bottled drinks from Lhasa or Shigatse.

Sights

Background For centuries, yak caravans loaded with bags of sheep and yak wool made their way from the northern plateau to Gyantse. Throughout Tibet's history, wool was its chief export. Gyantse's traditional caravan trade routes to Nepal and China were abruptly superseded by a new one to India in the early 20th century when Britain forced a trade agreement on Tibet (p.123). After 1959, Tibet's trade was re-routed through Lhasa and Gyantse lost importance.

Gyantse was a prominent trading centre by the 15th century. Its lords married with other noble clans of Tsang and founded Palkhor Monastery in a natural bowl of Gyantse's high, rocky spine. Its cosmopolitan character was reflected in a Nepalese-style stupa, the Kumbum, erected in 1427, and in the Chinese-style fortified wall protecting the whole monastic complex.

Gyantse also lay in the way of invasions from the south. Its citadel, the *dzong*, and its mini Great Wall withstood attacks by Nepalese Gurkhas, Sikhs and Ladakhis. Only when modern weapons overpowered Tibet's medieval army did Gyantse fall to a foreign power — the British in 1904.

The Kumbum

This spectacular stupa temple, whose name means "Place of a Thousand Images", was the centrepiece of Palkhor Monastery and the pride of Gyantse. A new road on the west edge of Gyantse leads straight to it.

It is the largest stupa in Tibet, built in 1427 by a prince of Gyantse. The great pagoda has a massive base consisting of four tiers of interlocking, multi-faceted chapels. Above it, a tall cylindrical section corresponds to the more common dome of most stupas and contains four large chapels. Over this rises a shaft with all-seeing eyes on its four sides in typical Nepalese style, plus a gilded tower with 13 rings, a parasol of filigreed metal and, at the top, a series of gold finials.

The Kumbum is the finest example of 15th-century Newari art extant in the world. The Newar people of Nepal's Kathmandu Valley, especially their fresco painters, were honoured and much sought after as artists in Tibet. Even today, Nepalese artists help to restore Tibet's monuments (p. 171).

On the lowest floor, four lofty chapels with restorations of indifferent quality mark the cardinal points. Sixteen smaller chapels, squeezed between them at sharp angles, provide many examples of the superior Newari art. Each of these chapels contains one dominant sculptured figure and elaborate, thematic murals. Those dedicated to sublime deities like Tara are beautiful. Others are awesome. A few display cruelty and terror. Pilgrims progress through them all, ascending clockwise through the different levels of the stupa to the top in a symbolic journey upwards to Nirvana.

Stupas

One of the most ubiquitous structures throughout the Buddhist world is the stupa: a round dome or cylinder on a (usually) square base, with a shaft or spike emerging upwards. The stupa is as fundamental a symbol to Buddhists as the cross is to Christians.

Stupas probably evolved in India from prehistoric times as burial mounds for local rulers and heroes. Legend says that in the 5th century BC Sakyamuni, the historical Buddha, asked to have his ashes interred in a stupa. With the launching of the new religion, stupas became formalised objects of worship. King Ashoka of India (273-232 BC) built innumerable stupas as an act of piety and to gain religious merit.

In early Buddhist art, Sakyamuni was never portrayed in human form, since the state of Buddhahood was considered indescribable. Instead, a stupa became the Buddha's symbol, a reminder of his earthly existence and a place of devotion. Stupas were erected by pilgrims in places where the main events of his life took place. Stupas became the main cult objects in monasteries where they were used to hold the mummified bodies or ashes of saints, like the tombs of the Dalai Lamas in the Potala, or to hold sacred objects, relics or scriptures. They were built to commemorate events, like the founding of Drepung Monastery on Gyengbuwudze Mountain, or to mark the place where a deity or a saint, like Atisha, was said to have lived.

The shape of stupas was adapted to local architecture wherever they spread and came to include a huge variety of types. The slender pagodas of China and Japan evolved from earlier, squat stupas. Sizes could range from tiny, ritual altar stupas to the former West Gate of Lhasa (now gone) whose base arched over a main thoroughfare. Yet all kept the same basic components.

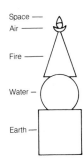

Space —
Air —
Fire —
Water —
Earth —

The different parts are associated with the elements: the base standing for earth, the dome for water and the shaft for fire, topped by a half-moon for air and a sun for infinite space. The shaft is usually formed of 13 rings, which represent the 13 steps to enlightenment. Richly decorated stupa-tombs have a face of open grill-work on the dome if a mummified body lies inside. Stupas containing scriptures, charms or treasures are closed, but may have a niche for a statue.

Chorten is the Tibetan word for a stupa. It refers not only to recognisable stupas but also to any sacred protuberance — a rock, a cairn or a pile of *mani* stones, to be worshipped by circumambulation, clockwise, with the sacred object always on the pilgrim's right.

Palkhor (Baiju) Monastery

The monastery is located behind Gyantse's mountain ridge on the west. Only four buildings remain: the Kumbum; the main, three-storey chanting hall; a dormitory for the 17 monks; and a Thangka Wall where giant Buddha banners were displayed once a year.

Palkhor was founded in 1365 and housed about 1,000 monks, prospering from its fertile lands and good location for trade. It suffered much damage in recent times. Current restoration is poor but some original art remains in the chanting hall and some fine Bodhisattva statuary exists in the North and West Chapels. At the lower roof level, the walls of one chapel are lined with lacquered statues of seated saints showing marked Indian influence. On the top roof level, the North Chapel has a superb collection of 15 mandala murals, all 3 m. (10 ft.) in diameter and in good condition.

West of the front porch is a weird "chamber of horrors", its entrance a prelude to hell, its main figures covered up as too awful to be seen.

Gyantse County Rug Factory

On the east side of Gyantse, this Tibetan rug factory continues a long tradition of Tsang rug making. Carding, spinning and dyeing of wool are done on the premises. Modern technology extends to treadle spinning wheels and electric finishing scissors. 1m. × 2m. (3 ft. × 6 ft.) rugs of good quality with bold, bright designs cost Rmb. 660 a pair.

The Dzong

Gyantse's fortress was stormed and partially destroyed by British artillery in 1904 (see next page). Subsequent damage in the 1960s left it in ruins. At the top of cliffs, protected by high castle walls, it contained a small monastery, garrison quarters and at its highest point, a cluster of elegantly placed apartments. A short distance from the Rug Factory, a steep, scrambling path leads up to the main portal. A crew of resident caretaker-restorers claims to require a special permit for entry but has been known to accept a small donation instead. The view over the town and valley is superb.

Yadong

Five kilometres south of Gyantse a road branching left leads 213 km. (132 miles) to Yadong near the Indian border. This beautifully situated Himalayan town has a mild climate, marvellous mountain views and forests. It boasts a fine, wooden, Sikkimese-style monastery 11 km. (7 miles) south on the border. Yadong is the gateway to Bhutan and India.

Britain Invades Tibet

Unlikely as it seems, Gyantse briefly became a household name in England in 1904 when, through a series of bungles, Britain invaded Tibet. In 1902, sudden, unfounded rumours claimed that China had offered mineral rights and other concessions in Tibet to the Tsar of Russia. The British Empire reeled and India's alarmed Viceroy sent a young diplomat named Francis Younghusband to the Tibetan border to find out the truth. The Tibetans, who had long since sealed themselves off from the world, were so suspicious of foreigners that they refused to talk to the British diplomatic mission.

Seeing this as a snub, London authorised Younghusband to march in with British troops as far as Gyantse, show the flag and force the lamas into an English-style agreement opening up trade between Tibet and India. Younghusband was given the instant rank of colonel, four artillery pieces and 1,000 soldiers under a bone-headed brigadier-general. This small army entered Tibet's Chumbi Valley in the December snow of 1903 accompanied by 1,450 coolies, 7,000 mules, 3,451 yaks, six camels and several foreign correspondents from London newspapers. The troops were served turkey and plum pudding for Christmas, though the frozen champagne was undrinkable. Then the cold, hunger, altitude and illness brought misery and deaths.

Tibetan troops armed only with muzzle-loaded muskets and magic charms against foreign bullets gathered near Gyantse. Younghusband, anxious to avoid bloodshed, made a bold, informal visit by night, alone, to the amiable Tibetan general to explain his mission. But angry lamas, who made policy, demanded immediate British withdrawal. The British proceeded towards Gyantse. When the two armies met, shooting began by mistake. In a four-minute massacre, 700 Tibetans were left dead or dying and the living walked slowly from the battlefield in sorrow and disbelief. Their bafflement only increased when a British Army field hospital tried to save the wounded and gave treatment to any Tibetan who asked for it.

At Gyantse the British captured the fortress and the Tibetans were decimated in one-sided battles. London sent an ultimatum to Lhasa. There was no reply. In August, 1904, Younghusband marched into Lhasa only to find that the Dalai Lama had fled to Mongolia. He forced a treaty on the Regent, giving Britain exclusive privileges, and withdrew.

At Gyantse, Britain established a flourishing Trade Mission. The next time Tibet was invaded (by China in 1910) the Dalai Lama fled to India as a guest of the English. Francis Younghusband, on his last night in Lhasa, had a deep religious experience that changed his life. He resigned and from then on devoted himself with great ability to humanitarian works.

The Yarlong Tsangpo River

The Yarlong Tsangpo, Tibet's principal waterway, is the upper half of India's great Brahmaputra River. It is 2,900 km. (1,800 miles) long from its source in western Tibet to its mouth in Bangladesh. "Tsangpo", appropriately, means "mighty". The Yarlong Tsangpo is the highest river in the world with an average altitude of 4,000 m. (13,000 ft.). It flows from west to east parallel to the Himalaya Mountains on their northern side.

Cascading from a high glacier, gathering snow water, the Yarlong Tsangpo enters a long, flat valley above Shigatse as a typical "braided" river winding among sandbanks. It flows through temperate, fertile Central Tibet to Tsedang where the river nurtured Tibet's first civilisation. Along the 650 kilometres (400 miles) of its middle reaches, a wide, navigable channel, shifting with the seasons, is plied by river craft — passenger and cargo boats driven by converted tractor engines; oblong, wooden "box boats"; and round coracles made of yak hide and willow boughs.

In eastern Tibet, the snow-capped massif of Namcha Barwa, 7,756 m. (25,447 ft.) high, blocks the river's eastward progress, forces it into a dramatic hairpin bend and drives it south to India, where it is renamed the Brahmaputra ("Son of Brahma, the Creator"). Here it turns west, crossing the Assam plain for hundreds of miles, parallel to its course through Tibet but in

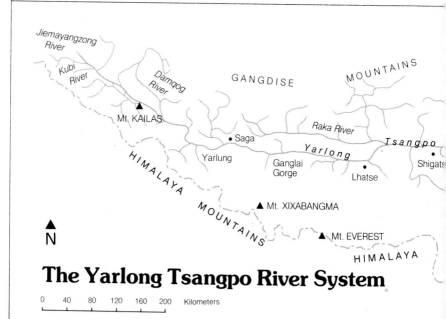

The Yarlong Tsangpo River System

0   40   80   120   160   200   Kilometers

the opposite direction and on the south side of the Himalayas. Its waters finally merge with those of the Ganges in a vast delta flowing south to the Bay of Bengal.

For a long time the Yarlong Tsangpo's source remained a mystery for western geographers. An Indian named Kinthup, one of the intrepid surveyor-spies employed by the British in the 1800s (p.46), first traced it to the sacred Kailas range of western Tibet. In 1904-5, after Colonel Younghusband had forced Tibet into cordial relations with British India (p.123), four British Army surveyors recorded their journey up the river from Shigatse through formidable terrain and hardships to confirm its source in a huge glacier near Mount Kailas.

Even more perplexing was its course through the eastern Himalayas, once people realised that the Yarlong Tsangpo and the Brahmaputra were one and the same river. They only knew that it entered the mountains on the north at 3,660 m. (12,000 ft.) and that it dropped an astounding 3,355m. (11,000 ft.) before emerging in India on the south. Excited geographers predicted an immense, hidden waterfall. Explorers finished their work in 1924 but found no falls higher than 9m. (30 ft.). Instead they discovered a series of incredible rapids and cascades, whose violent waters raced 10m. (33 ft.) per second through towering cliffs and gorges, eroding the riverbed deeper and deeper into the limestone rock.

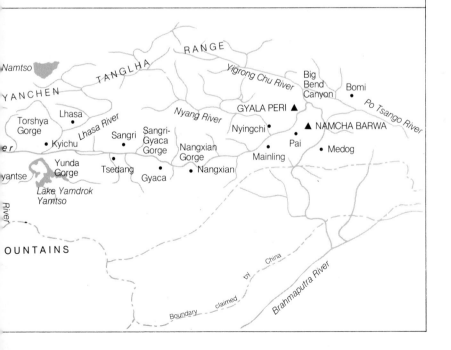

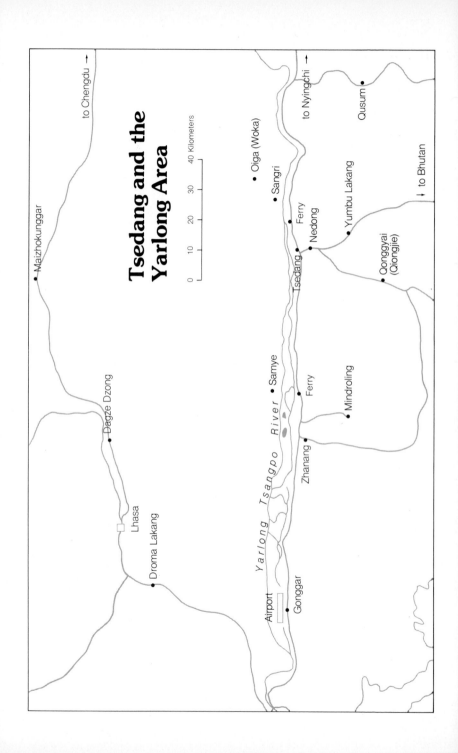

Tsedang and the Yarlong Area

0 10 20 30 40 Kilometers

to Chengdu

Maizhokungar

Dagze Dzong

Lhasa

Droma Lakang

Yarlong Tsangpo River

Airport

Gonggar

Zhanang

Ferry

Samye

Mindroling

Tsedang

Nedong

Ferry

Sangri

Oiga (Woka)

Yumbu Lakang

Qonggyai (Qiongjie)

to Nyingchi

Qusum

to Bhutan

Tsedang and the Yarlong Area

Southeast of Lhasa is a large administrative region known in modern times as Shannan ("South of the Mountains"). At its heart lies the ancient kingdom of Yarlong, the cradle of Tibetan civilisation. Tsedang, its capital, is at the foot of Mount Gongbori, one of Central Tibet's holy mountains. Tibet's creation myth tells how, in a cave at the back of this small mountain, a saintly monkey and an ogress gave birth to the Tibetan people (p.48). Their early history, including the reigns of some 30 half-mythical kings, unfolded in this section of the Yarlong Tsangpo Valley. Tsedang means "Playground", where the monkey came to frolic.

Tsedang (altitude 3,400 m. or 11,152 ft.) and the adjacent town of Nedong follow the familiar pattern: old, cosy Tibetan towns surrounded by the modern, utilitarian buildings of new, larger Chinese sections which, in this case, make them appear as one city, with a joint population of 25,000. Nedong, the smaller part, is the administrative capital of the Shannan area. Tsedang, which is socially and economically more important and growing fast, is a municipality. Both towns are small enough that a visitor can get around on foot for most purposes. The ruins of several monasteries can be seen in the old sections and the surrounding hills.

The outstanding physical features of Tsedang are the wide Yarlong Tsangpo River flowing just to the north of the city, Mount Gongbori overshadowing it on the east, and the profusion of trees all around that make Tsedang-Nedong an oasis in a strange, high-altitude desert.

Getting There

Officially, Tsedang and the Shannan area are only open to groups and people with special permission, not to visitors travelling with individual visas. Individuals requesting permission to visit the area (Visas, p. 32) get routine refusals from Lhasa's Public Security Bureau. However, there is some ambiguity in this situation. Travellers who make it to Tsedang without official permission usually find a warm welcome at hotels but risk expulsion back to Lhasa by the local Foreign Affairs Bureau.

Tsedang lies 190 km. (118 miles) from Lhasa, a four-hour drive. The road goes past the airport at Gonggar and continues east along the south bank of the Yarlong Tsangpo. It is surprising so close to the river to find that agriculture is sparse and that there are long stretches of desert. In places the stony mountains and sand dunes resemble a moonscape. Trees and irrigated fields of wheat and barley surround the occasional villages but the greenery soon peters out into faded plots and the drab desert once again takes over. Near Tsedang, planted forests of willow and poplar spread out from the river and agriculture picks up. This includes apple and pear orchards for which the region is famous.

Hotels

泽当饭店

Tsedang Hotel (Zedang Fandian) Planned and financed from Canton, it is the area's newest and best. Tsedang wants tourism and this 500-bed hotel is capable of handling foreign groups. It is located on Tsedang's main avenue, on the south side of town. The rooms are nearly all doubles, with western-style bathrooms. Hot water is produced by solar energy. It has a bar and three restaurants which boast chefs brought specially to Tsedang from China. The hotel has a fleet of 20 vehicles for sightseeing and day trips, at the usual CITS rate per kilometre. Price about Rmb. 100 per bed per day including three meals. Minimum Rmb. 30 per bed per day excluding meals.

泽当镇招待所

Tsedang Guesthouse (Zedang Zhen Zhaodaisuo) Adjacent to the Tsedang Hotel, this guesthouse is much simpler. Though mostly used by Chinese and Tibetan officials, the third floor is normally reserved for foreigners and well kept. Its l6 double rooms share a cold-water washroom and clean, Asian-style toilets. Beer and tinned food are available at a hotel store downstairs. One of its two dining rooms, for high-paying guests, offers a fixed Chinese menu. The other provides cheap, simple fare. Price Rmb. 90 per bed (third floor) per day, including three meals; Rmb. 6.50 per bed (dormitory) per day, excluding meals.

Sights

Background Archaeologists agree that the first agriculture in Tibet took place in the Yarlong region, confirming the Tibetans' own belief that their people, their culture and civilisation all originated here. Numerous other "firsts" are associated with Yarlong. The first known building still extant in Tibet lies just south of Tsedang. The first monastery was founded across the river nearby. Mythology places the first King of Tibet's arrival from the sky near Tsedang. The Kingdom of Yarlong was the heart of Tibet until the 7th century AD when King Songtsen Gampo moved the capital to Lhasa (p.48). Even thereafter, the kings' bodies were returned to Yarlong for burial in tumuli in the "Valley of the Kings", and they continued to look on it as their true homeland until the end of the monarchy in the 9th century.

Yumbu Lakang (Yongmu Lakang)

The castle of Yumbu Lakang is the oldest known dwelling in Tibet, reputedly the home of the Yarlong kings. It stands 12 km. (7½ miles) south of Tsedang, perched dramatically on a pinnacle above the valley. When the

monarchy ended, the castle became a small monastery. Smashed to rubble in the 1960s, it has been rebuilt. Original stonework in the lower part dates back at least to the 7th century.

History and myth are mixed for the 700 years of the Yarlong kings before Songtsen Gampo (617-649 AD). Legend ascribes the building of Ymbu Lakang to Nyatri Tsenpo, the first of the heavenly kings, who is believed to have descended from the sky around 130 BC. It is more likely that the castle was built in the 6th century during the reign of Songtsen Gampo's great-grandfather.

A steep track goes up from the road to the castle's base. Here, one can circle the building clockwise and avoid a steep flight of steps, while getting a fine view of the valley. The way leads in through a primitive kitchen and upstairs to a terrace. The small chanting hall has been richly redecorated under the supervision of five resident monks. A gallery above has interesting murals. One tells the legend of Yumbu Lakang's founding, with Buddhist details added from a later period. Different scenes show King Nyatri Tsenpo's arrival from the sky. He is carried on the shoulders of yak-herders to a white stupa (still standing across the valley) where he gives a sermon. Buddhist scriptures miraculously fall to earth. He founds a monastery on nearby Mount Shira (now destroyed), where a "sky burial" can be seen in the foreground. Then, realising he must stay on earth, he builds Yumbu Lakang as a home, thereby teaching Tibetans how to build houses. An adjacent mural has tales about the female deity Tara.

Samye Monastery

Tibet's first monastery is located north of the Yarlong Tsangpo River about 30 km. (18 miles) from Tsedang as the crow flies. However, a visit there takes a full day. To reach Samye, travellers leave their car at a ferry stop 36 km. (22 miles) west of Tsedang and cross the river in an open, flat-bottomed boat propelled by a converted tractor engine. The crossing may take an hour or more depending on the height of the water and position of the sandbanks. The ferry lands several kilometres upstream from Samye. The remainder of the trip is accomplished by tractor-drawn wagon over a very rough desert track, a 45-minute ride. All food and drink for the day should be brought from Tsedang.

The monastery, surrounded by a village, is in a green valley among barren mountains set back from the Yarlong Tsangpo. Haiburi, its small holy mountain, stands just to the east. Five ancient white stupas perched on crags overlook an early part of the trail from the ferry to Samye.

Samye Monastery was founded in 779 by Trisong Detsen, Tibet's "Second Religious King" (p.50), after he had invited prominent Buddhists to Tibet from India, the most famous of whom were Padmasambhava, the magician-saint (p.58), and Santarakshita, his personal tutor. The two teachers helped him found Samye as a school to train Tibetan monks, modelling it after a monastery in Bihar, India. Legends say Padmasambhava magically compelled Tibetan demons to haul stone and wood from rivers and forests each night so men could build the monastery by day, and forced the Nagas, the water-serpent deities, to give up their gold to finance the operation.

The first Tibetan monk, a Yarlong aristocrat who had attended a Buddhist university in India, was ordained by Santarakshita and installed as the first abbot of Samye. Santarakshita then ordained seven more nobles whom the king selected for their intelligence to receive this honour. Would-be monks came from far and near to be trained by them. The king enacted new religious laws placing monks above the royal law. Samye's abbot, entitled "Head of the Superiors", received more privileges than a minister of state. Certain landowning families of Yarlong were made subject to the monastery rather than the king and were obliged to provide the monks with food, income, butter, cloth, paper and ink, each according to his rank and degree. Anyone doing harm to a monk was severely punished — to a point where even a dirty look could mean having an eye put out.

In 791 King Trisong Detsen proclaimed Buddhism the official religion of Tibet, upon which two of his five queens and 300 other people promptly took religious vows and joined holy orders. Yet most of the aristocrats of Yarlong clung tenaciously to the old Bon faith. They hated the newly privileged class of Buddhist monks, which they saw as a mortal threat not only to the power of the nobility but to the monarchy itself. History proved them entirely correct. King Trisong Detsen grappled continually with the nobles. When he demanded that one of them build a stupa at Samye as an act of piety, the reluctant lord made it black, the colour of Bon.

Two divergent streams of Buddhism clashed at Samye. Chinese influence was as strong as that brought by Padmasambhava and Santarakshita from India. From 781 onwards, China sent two monks to Samye and replaced them every two years. Chinese Chan Buddhism, a forerunner of Zen, sought salvation through meditation and sudden insight, laying little store in ritual or good works. The Indians, on the other hand, embraced a moral code of good and bad deeds repayable in a future life, a slower route to salvation.

A great debate took place in the king's presence from 791 to 793. Two learned monks, one from China, the other from India, carried on a profound discourse whose text has been preserved. The Indian view triumphed and was adopted as the future course for Tibetan Buddhism to follow. Nonetheless, Chinese elements were incorporated into Lamaism. Many translations and catalogues of Buddhist texts were produced at Samye, and much scholarly writing was done during Trisong Detsen's time. But the

esoteric teachings of Lamaism were always transmitted by word of mouth, in the context of a strong, personal bond between teacher and pupil.

It took over a decade, 775-787, to build Samye, at the site of a temple founded by Trisong Detsen's father. Offerings from chief ministers and Trisong Detsen's five queens helped to pay the costs. At the centre was a large, three-storeyed hall surmounted by gold roofs, enclosed inside a protective cloister with elaborate gates at the cardinal points. Opposite the corners stood four big stupas, built by individuals in different pagoda styles, coloured red, white, green and black. Many surrounding buildings and temples completed the monastery. The whole was originally enclosed by a zigzag wall that was destroyed by fire. It was replaced in the 10th century by a great circular wall 3½ m. (12 ft.) high and 2½ km. (1½ miles) in circumference. Nain Singh, the surveyor-spy for the British (p.46), who stayed at Samye in the 1860s, gave an exact report of its physical features and its four large colleges. Photographs taken in the 1940s record its impressive layout, barely changed since the 8th century.

The architecture of the **Great Hall** combined styles that expressed the borrowings and mergings typical of Tibetan Buddhism. The lower part was constructed in the Tibetan manner, with two roofs, by builders from Khotan, beyond the Kunlun Mountains. The middle part was made in Chinese style, with three roofs, by Chinese carpenters. The upper part, also with three roofs, was built in Indian style by Indian craftsmen.

All that remains today is the Great Hall without its third storey and roofs, and the surrounding cloister, which houses 34 monks — 18 of them novices. The Great Hall faces east. The square cloister compound is entered by the east portal with its two stone elephants and giant bronze bell. Just inside is a huge prayer wheel under a canopy.

The main **Chanting Hall** has altar statues of five ancient historical figures: from left to right, a foremost translator of scriptures into Tibetan; an Afghan sage invited by the king to give guidance on Samye's construction; in the middle, with jewelled breastplate and popping eyes, an Indian exorcist, colleague of Padmasambhava, who rid the region of ghosts; King Trisong Detsen; and last, his ancestor King Songtsen Gampo. Butter and *tsampa* sculptures in glass cases, made at the Tibetan New Year, display excellent workmanship and show that this art form is still alive.

The West Chapel has a very large central figure of Sakyamuni that is made of stone beneath its garments. It dates from the 8th century. Only the head, recently destroyed, has been restored in clay. Pious Buddhists believe that the figure was formed naturally from Mount Haiburi's rock.

The North Chapel is a dark chamber whose three demon deities are considered so frightening that their heads are hidden under white scarves. Samye Monastery belongs simultaneously to three sects of Buddhism — the orthodox Yellow Hat sect and two of the unreformed Red Hat sects. The latter still contain strong elements of magic and demonology derived from the pre-Buddhist Bon faith, as is demonstrated here.

The South Chapel, with a separate entrance outside, has a memorable statue of Chenrezi with multiple heads and arms and 10,000 hands, in front of whom sits a fierce image of Padmasambhava (Guru Rinpoche).

Two upper levels of the Chanting Hall still contain some rare murals in spite of much damage. At the top, a pillared hall holds three statues of which Padmasambhava (centre) and Sakyamuni (right) are familiar. The left-hand statue is said to have come from the temple founded by King Trisong Detsen's father on this site before Samye was built. The modern pattern on its lap-robe adds an unexpectedly light-hearted touch.

The Roof offers a grand view over the village and countryside. A red, rounded structure to the southwest is the base of Samye's destroyed red stupa, which was considerably taller than the monastery.

The Cloister has living quarters for the monks on the upper tier. Below the gallery are remarkable murals, some original, some damaged, some restored. To the left of the portal on entering, beyond a row of prayer wheels, is a marvellously executed scheme of Samye Monastery as it was in the 8th century, complete with zigzag wall. Beyond it is a depiction of Chimphu Cave, an important Tantric centre northeast of Samye and still a sacred destination for pilgrims.

A major pilgrim path runs from Samye to Lhasa, a hard walking trip of four days and three nights. Experienced hikers who try it should take a tent as villages are scarce. There is plentiful firewood, fine scenery and occasional friendly nomads. Maximum altitude 4,850m. (16,000 ft.). The path ends at Dagze Dzong, 27 km. (17 miles) east of Lhasa.

How Buddhism Emerged in Tibet

Buddha means "The Enlightened One". Sakyamuni is a title of respect for the man named Siddharta Gautama who was born a prince in north India around 500 BC. He grew up in luxury, shielded from contact with human misery, and married young. One night curiosity led him outside, where he saw shocking examples of disease, old age and death. Determined to find a way to save mankind from suffering, Sakyamuni left his wife and child, renounced his princehood, and spent long years wandering as an ascetic. At last, fasting and meditating under a tree, he received enlightenment.

Buddha's insight into ultimate reality was embodied in Four Noble Truths and an Eightfold Path. He wished to be a guide, not an authority, and early Buddhism was a way of life rather than a religion. Its teaching encouraged people to take full responsibility for their thoughts and actions, on a path to spiritual growth.

Buddha's followers formed communities of monks and nuns, open to all, where they lived disciplined lives and sought wisdom, their prime virtue. For 500 years, while Buddhism spread throughout India, all the teaching was oral. In the 3rd century BC this early form of Buddhism, called Hinayana or the "Small Vehicle", took root permanently in Sri Lanka and spread outwards into other parts of South Asia.

In India, a new form of Buddhism appeared, called Mahayana or the "Big Vehicle", which appealed to many more people. Though sharing basic doctrines with Hinayana, its emphasis changed. Compassion was its chief virtue and its ideal was the Bodhisattva, a perfected individual who gave up heavenly bliss in order to return to earth and help humans.

Buddha was now treated like a god. Countless "mythical Buddhas" were

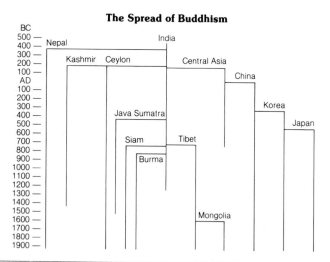

The Spread of Buddhism

invented to embody all of his aspects and their images were worshipped in temples. By the first century AD , scriptures, called sutras, laid down doctrines and monastic rules, and recorded Buddha's sermons as they were remembered. Mahayana Buddhism spread to China, Central Asia, Japan and on.

A third type of Buddhism saw man's harmony with the universe as the key to salvation. Adepts of Tantrism in India tried to manipulate external forces by magic, while followers of Chan in China induced inner harmony through meditation.

Buddhism died out in India around 1200 as Hinduism revived and harsh Moslem invasions destroyed its Buddhist centres. But their doctrines and scriptures lived on in Tibet, where Buddhism was promoted by the kings. The faith almost vanished with the end of the monarchy in the 9th century. When it arose again, Tibet's decentralised conditions allowed Lamaism to split into some 20 sects. The following five became the most important:

Nyingmapa, the "Ancient Ones", began around 750 with Padmasambhava. It absorbed the Bon faith and produced *The Tibetan Book of the Dead*.

Kahdampa began with Atisha after 1050. Its tradition laid stress on the scriptures and discipline and it formed a link with India's sages.

Kargyupta began around 1060 with the teachers Marpa and Milarepa. Most typically Tibetan in its methods, it stressed yoga as the way to seek enlightenment.

Sakyapa arose in 1073 at Sakya Monastery, which later governed Tibet. It was worldly and practical in outlook, less concerned with metaphysics.

Gelugpa, the "Virtuous Ones" or Yellow Hats, began with Tsong Khapa in 1407. It absorbed Kahdampa and carried on Atisha's tradition. It dominated Tibet after the 17th century, leaving other sects to play a minor role.

Major Schools of Tibetan Buddhism

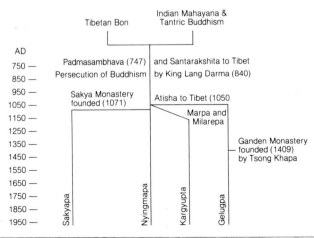

Mindroling Monastery

Tibet's only remaining Red Hat (Nyingmapa) monastery lies 54 km. (33 miles) west of Tsedang, a drive of 1½ hours. A small, sandy road turns south off the main road, 44 km. (27 miles) west of Tsedang. The right-hand road at a fork in the first village leads into a side valley where the monastery stands.

Nyingmapa means "Ancient Ones". It is the oldest, most unreformed sect of Tibetan Buddhism, founded in the 8th century by the Indian saint-magician Padmasambhava. It contains many elements of the pre-Buddhist Bon faith. As other sects proliferated and gained influence, the Nyingmapas remained strictly anti-establishment with no pretensions to political power. Their lamas were often married and lived in very small groups as hermits, Tantrists, yogis and sorcerers. They called themselves "madmen" and endeared themselves to the common people by their quizzical approach to life, their gibes at the excesses of the mighty, and their love of folklore and poetry. As "madmen" they sought access to the "Treasury of the Mind", their source of inspiration and creativity. They scorned books and declared learning useless, yet they produced an extensive literature.

Mindroling, meaning "Place of Perfect Emancipation", was founded in 1676 by Dieda-linba, whose ancestor was a famous Nyingmapa "Finder of Revelations". The teachings of this visionary had been carried on by his direct descendants for 300 years. Some of their doctrines were kept secret, especially their forms of meditation. Both the Second and Third Dalai Lamas are known to have studied these methods with Nyingmapa teachers. Dieda-linba became a tutor of the Great Fifth Dalai Lama who may have influenced him to found Mindroling as an orderly, monastic teaching centre. When the Great Fifth made the Yellow Hat sect supreme in Tibet by crushing rival sects, the Nyingmapas were ignored. Whether because it lacked wealth and posed no political threat, or because of the Dalai Lama's personal interest, Mindroling flourished.

Descendants of the Revelation-finder became abbots of Mindroling, succeeding one another from father to son, not by way of reincarnation. One son of the abbot would become a monk, vowed to celibacy (as were all the other monks), while another son, destined to be abbot, was expected to marry and continue the line. If he died, the monk brother was obliged to marry his widow. This has continued for over 20 generations; the present abbot lives in India.

Mindroling became the foremost monastery of the Nyingmapa sect — it is now the only one left. Almost as important, however, was Dorjetak Monastery near Gonggar. It was destroyed in the 1960s but may soon be rebuilt.

Mindroling and the village below it are built of finely dressed stone. The monastery formerly had many buildings around its large courtyard, including a five-storey stupa. It housed over 300 monks. The main chanting hall and a wrecked meeting hall are still standing, as well as living quarters for the four remaining monks and some 20 young novices. Restoration began in 1982.

The Main Chanting Hall, entered from the north, is dominated by a big statue of Dieda-linba, the founder, sitting in a glass case with fine, gilded woodwork. He is depicted in old age with the white hair and beard of a patriarch, wearing the red hat of his sect. On the east side of the hall is a collection of copper stupas filled with writings. The heavy bases are original, although some of the tops were damaged and recently replaced. On the walls, volumes of scriptures are wrapped in red, not the prevalent yellow of the Dalai Lamas. Extensive *tsampa* and butter sculpture graces the altar. A throne awaits the abbot's return from exile in India.

The South Chapel contains a giant statue of Sakyamuni holding a black bowl of clear water in front of a sculpted backdrop of mythical characters and beasts. Eight tall, androgynous figures represent Bodhisattvas.

The Chanting Hall's Roof has two levels. On the lower is a chapel with a gilded Tara and over 100 small copper stupas and figures behind wire netting. Some of these are magnificent, with details that deserve a careful look. On the upper level is a chapel with extraordinary murals, mostly originals, depicting all the important lamas ever to have lived at this place. All different, they display many personalities and degrees of magical power. The Sakyamuni in a glass case on the altar is said to be 300 years old.

Homeward bound; yak transport, Eastern Tibet

King Gesar of Ling

England has King Arthur and the Knights of the Round Table. India has Rama, in the tales of the Ramayana. Tibet has a beloved epic hero named King Gesar of Ling, who lives on in a host of songs and stories.

Tibet's popular literature has been overshadowed by a wealth of philosophic and religious writings. Yet a lively oral tradition existed among common folk outside of the monkhood which included songs, jokes, poems, proverbs, lampoons — and, above all, the stories of Gesar.

There are many versions but all agree that Gesar came to establish order on the earth and bring an end to injustice and violence. The tales were chanted by wandering bards of nomadic origin who spread them throughout Tibet. No bard knew them all but each had his own repertory which he chanted at gatherings or festivals. Most would deny that they had learned the poem by heart, insisting that they were inspired by Gesar himself, or some other divinity, who put the words into their mouths.

There may have been a historical king named Gesar. The songs place his country of Ling in the north, although the customs described are those of eastern Tibet. Some episodes originate in the old, magical Bon faith. Others are borrowed from Chinese or Indian folk tales. But as Buddhist thought permeated Tibet, Gesar became the incarnation of a Bodhisattva, sent to earth by Padmasambhava to fight the demons that gripped mankind. Gesar was born miraculously to a beautiful Naga water sprite who worked in the service of a king. People believed, therefore, that the boy was a prince. Gesar made a bargain with Padmasambhava before accepting his mission on earth. One condition was that he should have a brave uncle who was a good strategist. Something went wrong, and Gesar was saddled with a cowardly, miserly, greedy, treacherous step-uncle named Todong who is a stock character in all the stories, offering comic relief and a raw, human touch. Todong and the jealous Queen tried every means to kill Gesar but the boy always escaped. They finally banished him to Tibet's high wilderness, where he learned the skills of the nomads. When the old king died, Gesar returned and won a horse race in which he outwitted Todong and won not only the crown but a beautiful, loyal wife as well.

Gesar and his army undertook many campaigns against demons, giants and evil kings. His bold adventures were touched with high drama and romance. In the end he established order and justice on earth, and even made peace with Todong, who had become a buffoon in his old age.

His work done, Gesar retired to a mountain cave to meditate, and from there passed on to the mythical land of Shambala. Many Tibetans believe that he will come again. They say he will return with his army when Tibet is in great trouble and Buddhism is dying, to take vengeance on its enemies and once more usher in an era of peace and justice.

Valley of the Kings

Eight large mounds of earth resembling natural hills are believed to contain the tombs of Tibet's later kings in a valley 27 km. (16 miles) south of Tsedang. The road follows a river to the town of Qonggyai (Qiongjie) and enters the valley one kilometre beyond the bridge.

The biggest tumulus, on the right, is ascribed to King Songtsen Gampo (7th century AD). Steps lead up the side to a charming little temple on top. The temple was rebuilt and its murals restored in 1983. Three monks care for it and tend the flowers and apple trees in its courtyard.

The temple is dedicated to Songtsen Gampo, who was declared by the Fifth Dalai Lama to be an incarnation of Chenrezi, the Bodhisattva of Compassion, 1,000 years after his death. His statue is seated on a painted chest at the centre of the altar. Beside him, his Chinese wife, Wen Cheng, holds a Buddhist wheel of life, and his Nepalese wife, Tritsun, holds a crystal ball. Wise ministers stand on either side. Sambhota, the philologist who created Tibetan writing, is on the right, holding a book. A chapel behind the altar has a large, crowned Maitreya flanked by two Sakyamunis. The mural on the right wall depicts an Indian sage and attendant deities contemporary with King Trisong Detsen (8th century AD).

Some scholars doubt that Songtsen Gampo's body actually rests inside this tumulus, which has not been excavated, and suggest he was interred at the Jokhang in Lhasa. However, if ancient annals are to be credited, a rich,

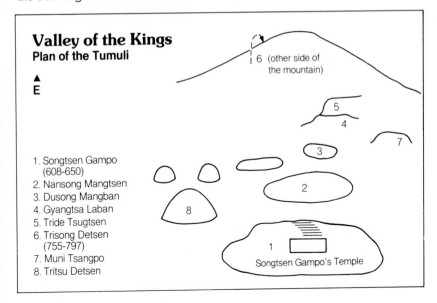

Valley of the Kings
Plan of the Tumuli

▲
E

6 (other side of the mountain)

5
4
7
3
2
8

1. Songtsen Gampo (608-650)
2. Nansong Mangtsen
3. Dusong Mangban
4. Gyangtsa Laban
5. Tride Tsugtsen
6. Trisong Detsen (755-797)
7. Muni Tsangpo
8. Tritsu Detsen

1
Songtsen Gampo's Temple

elaborate tomb lies below, with an internal configuration of symbolic importance. The king's body was reputedly placed in a silver coffin in a central, subterranean chamber, while nine smaller chambers were filled with vast treasures. (Nine and 13 were sacred Bon numbers.) Funeral rites included the sacrifice of men and horses who were buried with the king. The architectural layout made the tomb into a magical projection of the world with the king's body at the centre, holding its axis in place for eternity. The treasures piled up inside guaranteed the continuing prosperity of the kingdom.

Songtsen Gampo's reign marks the line between Tibetan mythology and recorded history. Very little exists to give us information about the kings who preceded him. The annals indicate that there were more than 30, in several lines or dynasties. Each one was said to have made discoveries and inventions that benefited the Tibetan people. Organised agriculture, a system of law, bridge-building, irrigation, charcoal, Chinese science and military skills consequently all made their appearance in Yarlong before the 7th century.

The first seven kings left no traces on earth, for they were not kings so much as gods exercising an earthly function. The king descended from the sky on a rainbow sky-rope to rule by day, returning to his heavenly home at night. As soon as his son learned to ride a horse, around the age of 13, he departed for good. This first royal line ended when the king arrogantly fought a duel without his magic weapons and accidentally cut his rainbow sky-rope. He was the first one to leave a corpse (which was put into a river) and thereafter the kings lived out their lives as humans. The early kings disposed of their dead in various ways, according to the practice of their dynasty. Royal remains were put in vessels and sarcophagi, or in rivers, or were dismembered for "sky burial". By Songtsen Gampo's time, burial in tombs beneath tumuli was an established custom.

The eight kings of the Tubo line whose tumuli fill the Valley of the Kings were all warriors. From their small base in Yarlong they kept up a series of huge military enterprises for almost 200 years. Military and civil administration were one and the same in Yarlong. Agriculture occupied the Tibetans for the summer season and the rest of the year was taken up with warfare. It happened that all of Tibet's neighbours suffered from internal disruptions which made them easy prey. Each territory conquered produced new skills and methods which Tibetans were quick to absorb. Skilful alliances furthered their success. Tibet under the Tubo kings became one of the mightiest powers of Central Asia.

Campaigns took Tibetans from the capital of China to Samarkand, where Arabs told them about the other empires of Byzantium and Rome. (One scholar has even suggested that Gesar's name was a Tibetan version of Caesar.) When Tibet slid down from this pinnacle, the descent was swift.

King Lang Darma turned the war machine against his own people in a furious effort to stamp out Buddhism. When his short reign ended with murder in 842, he had wiped out the monarchy and Tibet's role as a conquering power.

Changzhu Temple (Photographs are forbidden inside)

Very little remains of this ancient monastery in Changzhu village, 5 km. (3 miles) south of Tsedang on the road to Yumbu Lakang. It is thought to have been founded in the 7th century, during the reign of King Songtsen Gampo. The original temple was made of wood and thatch. In the 14th century it was rebuilt, enlarged and turned into a monastery. Further improvements were made by the Seventh Dalai Lama in the 17th century, at which time Changzhu supported 300 monks. The monastery contained numerous halls, including a Great Hall that was said to resemble the Jokhang. It was famous for its huge bell and sublime statuary. Although small, the monastery owned a disproportionate number of masterpieces of Buddhist art.

In the forecourt of the monastery, the immense beams and massive pillars of the 14th-century entrance can still be seen. One small temple stands in the inner courtyard. The only object of interest inside is its centrepiece, a banner embroidered with almost 30,000 pearls, representing Chenrezi in repose. The style is Indian and it is undoubtedly very old, saved from a monastery in Nedong that has been razed. Changzhu Temple is now the repository for a hodgepodge of saved religious objects gathered from various parts of Tibet.

Restoration began in 1982. A new dormitory for the seven resident monks and another "religious building" are being constructed from scratch. The forecourt has great historical value and deserves restoration but the murals have been so badly obliterated that it is doubtful any contemporary restorer could approximate the originals.

Nedong Carpet Factory

This small, primitive factory, hidden behind mud-brick walls on the south side of Nedong, is worth a visit from anybody interested in rugs. The factory does all preliminary work on the premises — carding with wire hand-brushes, spinning with treadle spinning wheels and hand dyeing in large vats. It employs 56 workers of whom 22 are weavers. The rugs are mostly of the common 1m. × 2m. (3 ft. × 6 ft.) size, destined to be sold in Tibet. Although most of the products carry typically bold, bright designs featuring flowers and dragons, here also can be found such rarities as the 700-year-old checkerboard design and a esoteric design of old Lamaist symbols in muted shades of beige and black.Unfortunately, the owners are normally unwilling to sell rugs to passing individuals, but an occasional visitor has been lucky, with rugs costing Rmb. 650 a pair.

Tsedang Primary School

Situated on the edge of Tsedang's old Tibetan quarter, this school has become a Chinese model for teaching the children of its "national minorities".

It was established in 1982, the outgrowth of an agricultural commune school, when money became available to improve Tibetan schools. It has six grades where Chinese and Tibetan children, in roughly equal numbers, study both languages while following an otherwise standard Chinese primary curriculum. Foreign tourists can visit the school by arrangement with CITS and see the classes in action.

Two Walks in Tsedang

There is not much to do in Tsedang when sightseeing tours are over, but with the relatively low altitude, walking is pleasant and easy.

The River Walk By walking north on the main avenue where the two tourist hotels are located, you soon come to the edge of the town. A small, sandy road leads north towards the Yarlong Tsangpo River between fields of barley and vegetables, ending after about 2 km. (1¼ miles) at a small village. Paths lead beyond it through groves of willow trees to the water's edge. A stroll along the riverbank at sunset can restore the most jaded spirits. Round-trip hike about 6 km. (3¾ miles).

The Hill Walk The destination of this walk is a tiny monastery hidden on the flank of Mount Gongbori. Walk north from the tourist hotels on the main avenue and turn right to Tsedang's old Tibetan quarter. (In many ways this is still a farm village in spite of urban surroundings.) A dusty road leads uphill past the ruins of Gajiu Monastery to a point where a shrine with many prayer flags can be seen on the mountainside a few hundred metres ahead on the right. A well-worn path goes to a water-source where women and children gather with their water pots. A path leads past the shrine, which consists of a big pile of stones and the mass of prayer flags, then around a shoulder of the mountain to tiny Sangga Singdzing Monastery. Here, an old lama, two monks and a young nun keep a little temple that is not included on any sightseeing tour. There is a fine view over Tsedang. Local pilgrims seem proud to show off this holy place of their own. The pilgrim path continues for a short distance beyond the temple to a square, white shrine, then circles back to the old town. Round-trip hike about 4 km. (2½ miles).

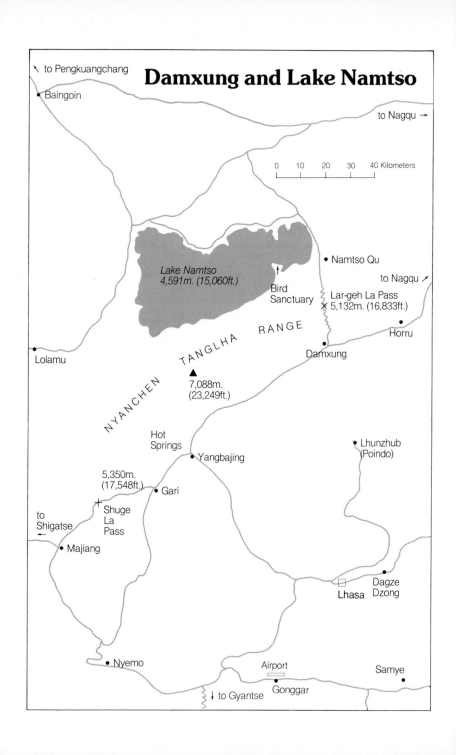

Damxung and Lake Namtso

to Pengkuangchang

• Baingoin

to Nagqu →

0   10   20   30   40 Kilometers

Lake Namtso
4,591m. (15,060ft.)

• Namtso Qu

to Nagqu ↗

Bird
Sanctuary

Lar-geh La Pass
✗ 5,132m. (16,833ft.)

TANGLHA   RANGE

• Horru

Lolamu

NYANCHEN

Damxung

▲ 7,088m.
(23,249ft.)

Hot
Springs

• Lhunzhub
(Poindo)

• Yangbajing

5,350m.
(17,548ft.)

✛ Shuge
La
Pass

• Gari

to
Shigatse
←

• Majiang

□
Lhasa

Dagze
Dzong

• Nyemo

Airport
▭
Gonggar

Samye

↓ to Gyantse

Damxung and Lake Namtso

A visit to Namtso, Tibet's largest salt lake, involves a two-day round trip from Lhasa of 420 km. (260 miles) and an overnight stay in Damxung. It is a fairly rugged trip, off the beaten track, but for those who enjoy roughing it the rewards are considerable. At present this is the best opportunity open to travellers to see nomads on the move with their yak herds and to get the flavour of Tibet's high grazing lands. The lake itself is spectacular and still totally wild.

The altitude exceeds 4,300 m. (14,100 ft.) for most of the journey and one mountain pass is around 5,200 m. (over 17,000 ft.) so warm clothes are essential. A windproof, waterproof outer garment and gloves are advisable. The weather is subject to abrupt, unpredictable changes and it is not uncommon to encounter a snowstorm on the pass between Damxung and Lake Namtso even in midsummer. Some tinned food and soft drinks should be brought from Lhasa, enough for two meals. Beer can be bought in Damxung.

Getting There

The road from Lhasa to Damxung follows Tibet's main route to Golmud and Qinghai for 167 km. (104 miles). Lake Namtso lies about 40 km. (25 miles) further, on the far side of the Nyanchen Tanglha mountains. A rocky, mountain track, requiring a vehicle with four-wheel drive, leads over a high pass and crosses the flat grassland near the lake.

After leaving the road junction 11 km. (7 miles) west of Lhasa, the route follows the Damxung River valley north through fields of rape and barley, passing small villages. Greenery and dwellings become sparser as the valley narrows. The road enters a steep, rocky gorge, 80 km. (50 miles) from Lhasa, and climbs beside the tumbling river for several kilometres. When it emerges on Tibet's northern plateau, a totally new landscape greets the traveller. Windswept grasslands alternating with gravel desert stretch between snowcapped mountains and a chain of steep, bare hills. This is the land of nomads, too high now for farms and villages. Settlements are few and far apart but the first town is reached almost immediately.

Yangbajing

This "electricity town", built around a thermal power plant, is 87 km. (54 miles) north of Lhasa, half way to Damxung. The altitude is 4,300 m. (14,100 ft.). Yangbajing borders on a flat area of hot springs covering 16 sq. km. (6 sq. miles). Steam and geysers, and a few drilling rigs, can be seen rising from the plain. If nomads are in the vicinity, yaks graze right up to the wire fence, apparently unperturbed by the racket of gushing steam and modern technology on the other side. The sprawling town on the left of the road consists of housing and private facilities for workers at the power plant. A roadside village next to it provides services for truck drivers who stop at this junction on the northern route to Shigatse.

The power plant, which supplies a large part of Lhasa's electricity, is the first and biggest thermal development in China, established in 1976. The electricity produced is vital to Tibet's economic development as all other kinds of fuel, except yak dung and wood, have to be trucked into Tibet from long distances. The plant can be visited by arrangement with CITS. A technician answers questions and conducts a guided tour of the steam-powered generators, cooling towers and steam-heated greenhouses where vegetables grow throughout the year.

The road runs northeast from Yangbajing through a long, straight, upland valley that is usually dotted with nomad encampments and herds of yaks. The nomads who roam over vast areas of northern Tibet make up about a quarter of the population. They produce the wool that has been Tibet's chief export for centuries and contribute an essential part of the country's diet in meat and dairy products. It is hard to be precise about their numbers as nomads sometimes live a half-settled life, especially in eastern Tibet. One tribe with the same name and same chief may be engaged in two entirely different occupations, sharing and exchanging roles as farmers and shepherds. Some nomads have fixed winter homes where they return for a few months a year. Others scarcely see four walls during their whole lives.

Nomads are big, handsome people — tough, cheerful and independent. At sacred places throughout Tibet they stand out in their sheepskin *chubas* (long coats) as the most ardent and joyous of pilgrims. They put high value on honesty and can dispense rough justice. It is said that nomads always return a kindness twofold but that they also repay a bad turn twofold.

Nomads live with family or relatives in easily movable black tents made of yak-hair felt. Tents invariably contain a fire-pit for cooking and an altar. Women and children usually work close to camp but men cover long distances alone on horseback. A typical family commands an impressive array of skills and can live for long periods without touching settled areas, their only outside essentials being tea and tsampa.

The animals — yaks, sheep and goats often numbering in the hundreds — are the family's private property. Men, women and children all use a sling and pebble with incredible accuracy to control the herd's movements, and dogs give some assistance, too. The woollen sling cracks like a whip as a pebble flies from its leather pouch and a moment later a straying yak can be seen galloping at full speed back to its herd.

Damxung

This bleak little settlement of low, barrack-like buildings is the administrative centre of Damxung County, founded in the 1960s. Its altitude is 4,400 m. (14,430 ft.). Damxung has no old Tibetan village at its heart like towns in the southern farming areas. Its main street has the raw look of an American Wild West frontier town, with stocky nomads' horses hitched to the posts of open-front stores. A small ghost-town stands near an abandoned airstrip. The wind never ceases and the treeless plain stretches unbroken to the distant mountains. The nearest towns are Yangbajing to the south, and Nagqu, 160 km. (100 miles) north.

Damxung is an important spot in this region for government functions and general supplies. It has a barn-like department store set back from the main street, where basic necessities and sturdy clothes can be bought. Open-front stores by the road sell items nomads like to buy, such as plastic flowers and plaster Buddha statues! Truckers stop here for gasoline and food. A major festival called Dajyur draws nomads to Damxung from all directions at the beginning of the lunar calendar's eighth month (solar September) for ten days of festivity, horse-racing, bicycle-riding contests, rock-carrying competitions and other forms of merriment.

Hotels

当雄招待所
Damxung Guesthouse (Dangxiong Zhaodaisuo)

This is the only place in town where a visitor can stay. It is located in the compound of the county headquarters. Its 20 rooms offer plain but adequate accommodation. There is no plumbing, but thermoses of hot water are provided for washing. An older wing also has guest rooms. Price Rmb. 2 — 5 per bed per day.

There is a dining room in the compound where foreigners can eat if the staff is informed in advance what meals are required. They will cook rice and whatever else is available in Chinese style and provide *mantou* (steamed bread) for a picnic at Lake Namtso. Tinned food is available in Damxung but the choice is limited.

The alternative place to eat is a small truck-stop restaurant on the right side of the road at the north end of the town. The premises are very primitive but the atmosphere is friendly. Rice or noodles are available, and usually two kinds of vegetable. The dried yak meat is inedible when stir-fried with vegetables, but it is not too bad when served stewed in a broth with noodles. A small shop across the road sells bottled beer and snacks.

Lake Namtso

A track from Damxung crosses the plain and follows a stream up a steep, rocky valley into the mountains. Local Tibetans say that wolf, bear and leopard still live in the Nyanchen Tanglha range. A stark crag etched against the sky and a stone pile bristling with prayer flags mark the top of the Lar-geh La Pass, 5,132 m. (16,833 ft.) high.

Occasionally, cars meet a caravan of several hundred yaks heading through the pass laden with hand-woven bags of sheep's wool. This is a wonderful sight. Steered by mounted, sling-wielding outriders and circling dogs, they fill the narrow passage. Although yaks look large and clumsy at first sight, they are surprisingly graceful on the move, trotting swiftly on dainty hoofs with their long hair flying.

Yaks are probably the most efficient, all-purpose animals in the world, supplying almost everything a nomad needs. They give butter, milk and meat for food, and wool for clothing and tents. Their dung, sun-dried into hard bricks, can be used as fuel or building material for wind-shelters. They provide transportation, as saddle or pack animals. Unfortunately, they are also extremely ill-natured and stubborn. But when bred with domestic cattle, their offspring is the versatile *dzo*, which is frequently seen in Tibet's valleys.

Just beyond the pass, a dramatic view opens over the boundless expanse. Bright, sapphire-blue, Lake Namtso stretches away to the southwest, 4,591 m. (15,060 ft.) above sea level. This is the second biggest salt lake in China (after Kokonor, or Qinghai Hu) with a surface area of 1,940 sq. km. (750 sq. miles). A nomad, moving steadily, needs 18 days to circle it. This part is its narrow, eastern tip. The road descends rapidly to the plain where it continues over the grassland, fording shallow streams. Mount Nyanchen Tanglha's white head soars 7,088 m. (23,249 ft.) in the west and the tin roofs of Namtso Qu, a tiny county station, can be seen near the foothills far off to the east.

To reach the lake's edge, a four-wheel-drive vehicle must leave the track and make its own way. Several kilometres west, a group of isolated hills extends into the lake. This peninsula is called Bird Island (Zaxi Dao) for the thousands of birds that are said to nest here. A deep cave also exists at this spot. With careful navigating and sufficient time, a jeep could probably reach it. For most people, an expedition to the closest part of the shore and a picnic are enough.

Water birds skim the brackish water and, in June, hundreds of wild geese nest close offshore on banks of reeds. Colour abounds everywhere, in tiny, jewel-like flowers underfoot and distant mountain rocks. To take a short walk and experience the immense distances, the timelessness and the total silence of the plateau is perhaps to understand the nomads' deep love for this land.

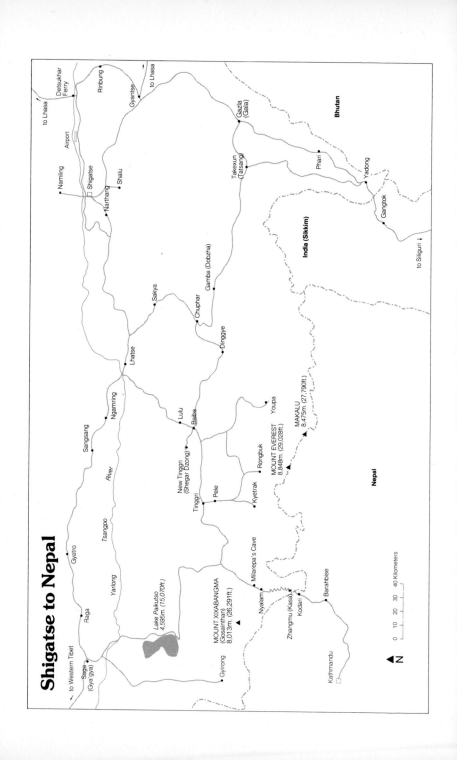

Shigatse to Nepal

Shigatse to Nepal

The only officially sanctioned, overland route for foreigners to take out of Tibet goes southwest from Lhasa, through Shigatse, to Zhangmu (also called Kasa) on the border of Nepal. This is a journey of 830 km. (520 miles). Lhasa's Public Security Bureau issues permission to visit Zhangmu without problem. Travellers intending to continue from Zhangmu to Kathmandu must have a Nepalese visa, which can be obtained at the Nepalese Consulate on Norbulingka Road, close to the Lhasa Hotel (Useful Addresses, p.202). The consulate issues visas from a special window by the gate, Monday-Saturday, 10:30 am to noon. The traveller needs an Alien's Travel Permit valid for Zhangmu and three photographs. A one-week visa costs Rmb. 35.

Travel in the reverse direction — from Kathmandu, through Zhangmu, to Shigatse and Lhasa — is at present limited to tour groups registered with CITS. However, CITS can change regulations at a moment's notice, so it is wise to get the latest up-to-date information from any of the tourist agencies in Kathmandu that arrange trips to Tibet. In general, however, it is more comfortable to take this trip leaving Tibet, when fully acclimatised, than entering it, because of the big changes in altitude on the route. The trip from Lhasa to Shigatse has been described on p.101. This section starts at Shigatse and proceeds southwest to Nepal.

Getting There

It is very hard to pick up transportation in Shigatse, so the whole trip to Zhangmu should be arranged in Lhasa. Individuals usually gather a group to hire a minibus together. CITS can provide vehicles more conveniently, though somewhat more expensively, and can arrange transportation beyond Zhangmu to Kathmandu.

The distance from Shigatse to Zhangmu is 530 km. (330 miles). It can be driven in one hard day, taking a picnic. There is also the possibility of spending a night in New Tinggri (also called Shegar) roughly half way, where adequate accommodation is available, or of roughing it in a smaller place.

The route crosses two major passes between Shigatse and New Tinggri (Shegar). The Tsuo La, 113 km. (70 miles) from Shigatse, is at 4,500 m. (14,760 ft.) and has a rugged, highland view. The Jia Tsuo La, 235 km. (147 miles) from Shigatse on open uplands, has a sign giving its height as 5,220 m. (17,122 ft.) but reliable maps indicate it is higher — 5,252 m. (17,226 ft.). Beyond Tinggri, the Lalung Leh Pass, 441 km. (275 miles) from Shigatse, has an altitude of 5,214 m. (17,102 ft.). It commands an incomparable view of the Himalayas in all their snowbound glory. From here the road descends rapidly for another 90 km. (56 miles), dropping 3,000 m. (almost 10,000 ft.) in two hours, down to the pine forests of Zhangmu.

Sakya Monastery (Admission Rmb. 3.)

This important old monastery, whose name means "Tawny Soil", governed the whole of Tibet in the 13th century, after the downfall of the kings. Its medieval Mongolian architecture is quite unlike that of monasteries in Lhasa or Yarlong. It is worth taking the time for a side trip off the main road to see it (2 hours for the round trip is enough).

Getting There

The turn-off to Sakya is on the left, immediately after crossing the Sakya River bridge, 128 km. (80 miles) west of Shigatse — 15 km. (9 miles) from the top of the Tsuo La Pass. A rough road leads down a long, dry valley for 26 km. (16 miles) to Sakya village. The forbidding, fortress-like monastery can be seen from a distance, looking like a single grey and red block with one horizontal white stripe.

Background Originally, the monastery stood in two parts, built at different times, on either side of the river. The first was founded in 1071 by a powerful noble family of Tsang. Its buildings, incorporating a cave, were piled against the mountainside east of the river in typical Tibetan style. The abbots were strong administrators and, since the succession passed from paternal uncle to nephew, power stayed in the hands of the founding family. Soon, the monastery controlled so much of Tsang province that the abbot needed assistance from a civil and military governor, quaintly entitled the "Great Hermit". Much scholarship was carried on, as Sakya owned a large trove of Buddhist texts, all that were left after India's libraries were burned down by Moslem invaders. A separate sect of Tibetan Buddhism took form here, named Sakyapa (p.139).

One abbot, Sakya Pandit, was such an outstanding scholar and debater that his fame reached Mongolia. In 1244, the son of Genghis Khan sent for him to be his teacher. In return, he granted the monastery provisional rulership over Central Tibet. Sakya Pandit took along his nine-year-old nephew, Phagspa, who was later to become Sakya's greatest abbot and the lifelong spiritual guide of Kublai Khan, the Emperor of China. Such was the influence of Sakya Monastery.

Sakya reached its heyday in the second half of the 13th century, when it was showered with gifts and privileges, and given control over all Tibet by Kublai Khan. In 1268, a new, more magnificent monastery was built across the river from the old one in purely Mongolian style. For almost a century Sakya remained the secular and religious centre of Tibet.

After Kublai Khan's death, Mongolian power waned. The Mongols abandoned Buddhism (the Third Dalai Lama later reconverted them) and

Sakya was overthrown by rival monasteries. Tashilhunpo, founded by the Yellow Hat sect in 1447, took over as the religious centre of Tsang.

Nothing remains today of the first monastery. It fell into disrepair by the 15th century and was demolished in recent times. High foundations built into the mountainside can still be seen across the valley.

Three buildings of the 13th-century monastery remain, protected by massive, windowless, fortress walls with corner towers — a typical Mongolian feature. Narthang Monastery (p.117) and Shalu, after the earthquake (p.115), were built along the same lines as Sakya. The grey and murky maroon hue of the outer wall appears drab but these two colours are favoured throughout the region, painted in stripes on village walls.

The monastery is entered on the west side. It includes the Main Hall, an East Hall and a dormitory building with a fine facade for Sakya's 30 monks. Much restoration and rebuilding is taking place among other structures which form a veritable village inside the bastion.

The Main Hall is constructed around an inner courtyard. The high ceilings and huge doorways of the entrance set an awesome, monumental tone that prevails throughout. Peeling murals of the Four Heavenly Kings in the vestibule were made by Mongolian artists in their own, distinctive style. The courtyard has high, decorated beams and woodwork, but no overhanging eaves or roof ornaments as are commonly seen elsewhere.

The Chanting Hall is wider than it is deep, with pillars made from whole tree trunks. Daylight entering from high windows illuminates a fine frieze of Buddhas, saints, guardians and Mongolian hierarchs, embellished by lion decorations, near the ceiling above the altar. Everything in the room is big — the monks' seats, a huge barrel drum, seven giant Mongolian-style Sakyamunis in golden settings. Gilded brass figures placed high on pillars and walls increase the sense of space. The central altar figure, wearing a red and silver Mongolian hat, is Kunga Nyingpo, a master scholar of Sakya's great period, equal in learning to Sakya Pandit. He organised a systematic teaching of the Tantras and is always portrayed as an old man. In front of the altar are some of Sakya's treasures — artifacts of silver, porcelain, ivory and shell. Jewelled stupas holding the ashes of the founders also indicate its former wealth.

The East Hall contains seven big, gilded stupas and three lesser ones. Restored murals show a giant portrait of Kunga Nyingpo with two equally big guardian deities filling a whole wall, and big, bold mandalas. It is very rare to see a portrait mural of these dimensions in Tibet. In a glass case beneath it is a mandala of coloured sand which the monks destroy and reconstruct once a year. An inner chapel contains six large, white stupas containing the remains of Sakya's early abbots.

New Tinggri (Shegar)

New Tinggri lies in a side valley north of the main road, 280 km. (175 miles) from Shigatse.

Getting There

After leaving the Sakya bridge, the next important settlement is Lhatse, a county seat and truck stop at the junction with the western road to Western Tibet and Kashgar. Taking the southern fork at the junction, the country soon becomes uninhabited and wildlife can sometimes be seen — musk hare, antelope, gazelle and a variety of birds, including wild geese. The road enters a long, rocky gorge and emerges on a desert plateau almost too high for grass to grow — only a thin layer of peat covers the barren soil. The Jia Tsuo La Pass would be imperceptible but for its rock piles and prayer flags.

Descending towards New Tinggri, the white range of the Himalayas is seen in the distance. New Tinggri is not visible from the road: it is necessary to go right, up a small valley. If you reach a security checkpost barring the main route, an unmistakable landmark, you have gone too far by several kilometres. All vehicles are required to stop at the checkpost and everyone must show their travel documents before being allowed to continue onward to Nepal.

Sights New Tinggri formerly had a fortress perched on the cliffs above and a monastery known as "Shining Crystal". Now the town is composed of an old Tibetan quarter and a larger Chinese section, where the guesthouse is located. Above the old village, part of the fortress wall with its tall towers marches up the mountainside from the ruins of the monastery to a bare pinnacle where the bastion's foundations remain. This beautiful spot, with a splendid view across the valley to Mount Everest, is worth the climb.

Hotel

The New Tinggri Guesthouse (Xin Dingri Zhaodaisuo) This guesthouse has about 20 rooms, each with three beds. There is no plumbing, but cold water taps are located close to the rooms for washing, and hot water is provided in thermoses. A restaurant serves good, but relatively expensive meals (there is also a small noodle restaurant in town, between the guesthouse and the Tibetan quarter). Price Rmb. 15 per bed per day.

Rongbuk

Formerly the site of the highest monastery in the world at 5,030 m. (16,500 ft.),

Rongbuk is now known as the starting point for climbing expeditions up Mount Everest. A fairly new road to Rongbuk turns south 11 km. (7 miles) west of the security checkpost. The old road, in poor condition, goes south from Tinggri, 48 km. (30 miles) further west. Both roads are sometimes broken by floods during the summer rainy season.

The stony valley of the Rongbuk River rises gradually, with Mount Everest filling the southern horizon. The ruined monastery at the head of the valley was formerly a supremely sacred pilgrimage site, housing over 100 monks. Wild animals, such as antelope, blue sheep and the Tibetan wild ass, were reported by the first English mountaineers to be abundant in the valley, and tame, because they had never been harmed. The monks tried to discourage Everest's climbers during the 1920s and 1930s, fearing that the spirits of the mountain would kill them; they depicted their imagined fate at the hands of angry gods, demons and snow leopards in mural paintings.

The monastery was destroyed some 20 years ago in the Cultural Revolution, and the growing numbers of international mountain climbers since 1975 have disregarded ecology by using its remains as a rubbish dump. The base camp of Mount Everest is 6 km. (3¾ miles) further up the slope, where the track beyond the monastery ends.

Tinggri

The town lies a short distance off the main road, 60 km. (37 miles) west of the checkpost. From here there is a spectacular view in clear weather to the peaks of Mounts Everest, Lhotse and Makalu, the highest group of mountains in the world. Mount Everest is on the right.

Tinggri used to be an important trading post where Sherpas from Nepal exchanged rice, grain and iron for Tibetan wool and salt. It gives its name to the broad, upland basin more than 4,500 m. (15,000 ft.) high that is known as the Tinggri Plain. At this point it is over 30 km. (20 miles) wide. Shallow, fast-running rivers of snow water make its grassy meadowland ideal for grazing.

Hotels

There are two very simple guesthouses with several beds to a room. Neither guesthouse has electricity or thermoses of hot water but they do offer a well for water, plenty of children and dogs, a friendly atmosphere and a fine view. One of them says it can provide food. Prices Rmb. 1 per bed per day.

Climbers of Mount Everest

Mount Everest reaches 8,848 m. (29,028 ft.) — nearly nine kilometres or five and a half miles high. English surveyors first measured the world's highest mountain in 1852 from the distant plains of India as Tibet and Nepal were both closed. They named it after Sir George Everest, a great English surveyor, not knowing it already had a name — Qomolangma.

For many years, John Noel, an English army officer, sought in vain for permission to visit the mountain. In 1913 he entered Tibet from Sikkim in disguise. He was discovered and turned back by armed Tibetans 64 km. (40 miles) from Everest but by then he had seen a great deal. His lectures in England aroused passionate interest among mountaineers. In 1920, Sir Charles Bell, Britain's political officer for Tibet, persuaded the Thirteenth Dalai Lama to let English mountaineers climb Everest.

A reconnaissance group retraced Noel's route. The first expedition, in 1922, included John Noel and George Mallory, the best climber of that era. (It was he who, when asked why he climbed Everest, gave the famous reply, "Because it is there."). After a month-long trek from Sikkim, they established a base camp at Rongbuk where they first heard about the yeti — a mystery that intrigued the whole world. They used oxygen but the climb was aborted by an avalanche that killed seven of their Sherpas.

Another expedition was mounted in 1924. Mallory and an able young companion, Andrew Irvine, were nearing the summit when John Noel, watching below, lost sight of them. They did not return and their bodies have never been found. The possibility remains that they might have reached the top and died on the return trip. There is no way of knowing.

Eight more expeditions attempted Everest from Tibet before the Second World War broke out. The greatest climbers in the world tried it, as well as amateurs. All were defeated by storms, snow and altitude.

When China closed Tibet in 1951, the British traced a new route up Everest through Nepal. In 1952, Swiss mountaineers very nearly succeeded but were halted by storms. A Russian team on the Tibetan side is believed to have lost six of its members on the mountain that same year.

On May 29, 1953, the peak was finally reached by New Zealander Edmund Hillary and Tenzing Norgay, a Sherpa who had climbed with the Swiss.

From that moment on, Everest became climbable. In 1956, four Swiss stood on top. In 1960, a Chinese team made it from Tibet. In 1963, six Americans took different routes to the peak. In 1965, nine Indians succeeded, followed, in 1975, by one Chinese and eight Tibetans. There were failures, too, but by the autumn of 1985, 179 individuals had stood on the world's highest point. Nearly 20 of them went up more than once, and the Sherpa Sungdare held the record, having climbed to the top of Mount Everest four times.

Nyalam

This little town of stone buildings and tin roofs is perched on a mountainside 35 km. (22 miles) from Zhangmu, at 3,750 m. (12,300 ft.). Two rivers meet here at the head of a precipitous gorge. Caravan traders from Nepal used to call it "The Gate of Hell", because the trail between Nyalam and the Nepalese border was so dangerous to negotiate. Bad weather or unforeseen circumstances occasionally cause travellers to stop here, though it is barely an hour's drive from Zhangmu.

Getting There

From Tinggri, the road loops around an impenetrable mass of Himalayan rock before it turns south. The Tinggri Plain becomes a windswept desert, with snowy peaks on all horizons. As the valley narrows, the road climbs ever higher to a wasteland of dry, gravelly hills. The only bright colour here is the green line of a stream winding down a shallow valley and the blue sky above. All else is tan, with the white heads of the Himalayas rising dramatically over the southern horizon.

The Lalung Leh Pass is defined by two scarcely noticeable high points, with a steep valley between them. It marks the edge of the wasteland and gives a breathtaking view of a whole range of the snowclad Himalayas. From here the road plunges through a crack in the mountains into a totally different climate. The effect of South Asia's monsoon could hardly be demonstrated more clearly than in the two-hour descent from the Lalung Leh Pass to Zhangmu.

Warm, seasonal, monsoon winds, laden with moisture, blow over India from the Bay of Bengal every June or July to start the "wet season". Rising to cross over the Himalayas, the air cools and drops torrential rain on the southern slopes which are consequently covered with forests or jungle. Scarcely a drop falls on the northern face, however, where lifeless, gravel desert stretches down from the snowline.

Beyond the pass, the road follows a rapidly falling river right through the Himalayas in a series of gorges, hugging the mountainside. Patches of barley edge the river wherever the ground is flat. Low, flowering shrubs start to appear among the rocks, then leafy plants, and finally tall wild flowers.

Hotels

Nyalam Guesthouse This simple hostelry is good to know about in an emergency, but is not particularly friendly. It is on the right side of the road entering the town. Price Rmb. 3 per bed per day.

Milarepa

Of all the religious masters and strange characters that have appeared in Tibet's history, Milarepa is the people's favourite. He was a combination of poet, eccentric, hermit, magician and saint, avocations that were much appreciated by Tibetans. An extraordinary, exuberant man, Milarepa left a legacy of many thousands of songs and poems, and a biography written by his chief disciple. In some ways his life resembled that of St. Francis of Assisi — a sinner in youth who repented, devoted his maturity to selfless works and ended his life as a beloved, revered saint. Mila was his family name. Repa means "cotton-clad", as, once he had become a hermit, he never wore more than a cotton cloth, despite the bitter cold.

He was born in 1040 to a family of comfortable means. His father died when he was seven. By Tibetan custom, the widow, her son and daughter and all the family property were entrusted to the father's brother until Milarepa came of age. This faithless uncle took the property for himself and forced the family to be his servants. Milarepa's mother possessed one asset — a plot of land in her own name, which she now sold to pay for a special education for her son. She sent Milarepa to learn black magic from a sorcerer so that he could wreak revenge on the uncle.

Milarepa succeeded brilliantly at his studies. He brought about the death of his uncle's oldest son (and several other people) by collapsing the roof of a house on to his cousin's wedding party. And he destroyed the uncle's crops with hailstones. Thus defeated, the uncle returned the patrimony. But Milarepa was overcome with remorse. He renounced worldly goods and went looking for a teacher who could lead him to the Light.

He went to Marpa (1012-1096), a fearsome, contradictory Tantric master who was violent and worldly yet a remarkable scholar and teacher. Marpa refused to take him as he could not pay, so Milarepa offered his own person, body and soul, and entered a long, cruel apprenticeship, designed to purge him of his sins, endlessly building and tearing down a tower. Satisfied at last, Marpa taught him, initiated him and sent him to a life of contemplation, rather than scholarship like his other disciples. He earned Milarepa's lifelong devotion, as many of the songs show.

Milarepa lived as an extreme ascetic. He ate nothing but nettles until his hair turned green, singing his joyful songs of praise and wisdom. He developed great occult powers and clairvoyance which he used, allegorically, in contests of magic to convince the Bon priests of Buddhism's superiority, or to perform his countless acts of kindness. Milarepa lived to the age of 83, a wise, inspired, compassionate madman who captured the hearts of all Tibetans. His images usually portray him smiling ecstatically, with his hand raised to his ear as he sings.

Milarepa's Cave

A cave where Milarepa spent many years of his life is 10 km. (6 miles) north of Nyalam between the main road and the river at a tiny village called Zhonggang. A path leads from the roadside through the village and down the hillside where a small monastery has recently been rebuilt on a terrace overlooking the river. The hermit's cave is entered from its vestibule. Pilgrims' offerings of decorated stones along the path and sweet-smelling herbs and wild flowers growing all around make this a spot of great peace and beauty.

The cave, which is quite small with a low, rock ceiling, is kept as a shrine by two monks. A statue of Milarepa in a glass case shows him happily listening to his own singing, but he has been uncharacteristically dressed in warm clothing.

The monastery, consisting of a small chanting hall and vestibule, is named Pyenzhangling, like a monastery that is consecrated to Milarepa in Nepal. A monastery had existed at the site of this cave since the 17th century, to take care of pilgrims, but it was totally destroyed in 1966. The restoration has all been done by Nepalese craftsmen and artists, with money supplied by the Chinese government.

Zhangmu (Kasa)

Although its name is missing from many maps, Zhangmu is considerably bigger than Nyalam. It snakes down a steep mountainside on both sides of the road above the Sun Kosi River, in sight of the Nepalese border. The road makes at least five hairpin turns back and forth through the town. Steps connect its different levels for hardy people on foot. By road it is about 4 km. (2½ miles) from the upper end of Zhangmu to the lower. The average altitude is 2,300 m. (7,544 ft.).

Getting There

The drive from Nyalam to Zhangmu through the gorge is an amazing experience. High cliffs enclose the rushing river. The road is sometimes high above it, sometimes close to the water. Scrub pine bushes appear near the upper end of the gorge and the riverbed is filled with mossy boulders. Trees grow thicker and taller as the road descends. Waterfalls cascade down the cliffs through green grottoes of fern and moss. The sight of so much lush greenery seems unbelievable after the bleakness of the high desert. Towering pine trees have formed a real forest by the time Zhangmu's roofs appear on the mountainside below.

Hotels

樟木宾馆
Zhangmu Hotel (Zhangmu Binguan) The only tourist hotel in the town. It lies below the road at the extreme lower end of Zhangmu and is entered by a footbridge at the top floor. The hotel was started in 1980 and opened to foreigners in 1984. It has 40 double rooms for foreign visitors on the second and third floors, with small balconies overlooking the valley. Each room has a western-style bathroom with its own electric water heater that works sporadically during the daytime. The hotel's electricity is turned off between 11 p.m. and 8 a.m. The hotel is somewhat pretentious and does not live up to its billing. There is no telephone connection to Lhasa or the outside world. Service is extremely poor. Payment for meals is illogical and the food is monotonous. The hotel only gets galvanised into action when a CITS tour group comes through, then everything, including the food, improves. Prices Rmb. 15 per bed per day.

接待办招待所
Reception Office Guesthouse (Jie Dai Ban Zhaodaisuo) This Chinese-style billet is an alternative to the Zhangmu Hotel. It is simpler and cheaper, located in the middle section of the vertical town. Rmb. 7 per bed per day.

Primitive though friendly accommodation can be found among the numerous teashops and huts that cling to the side of Zhangmu's only road. Prices are negotiable.

Exit Procedures

Chinese foreign exchange certificates should be redeemed for foreign currency before leaving the country. A branch of the Bank of China is located high above the Zhangmu Hotel. Tellers will ask to see passports and a receipt showing that the foreign exchange certificates were obtained legally. They will not give foreign currency for leftover Renminbi under any circumstances. Nepali rupees are used as soon as the Chinese customs post is passed, so it is advisable to get a few. (Rmb. 1 = approximately 7 Nepali rupees.)

There is a post office on the level above the bank, for final mailings from Tibet.

The Chinese border post, for passport control and customs, is next to the Zhangmu Hotel at the road barrier. The actual border is the Friendship Bridge over the Sun Kosi River several kilometres further on.

From Zhangmu to Kathmandu

The Chinese-built Friendship Bridge was washed away by floods in 1981. While its replacement is under construction, the river has to be crossed on foot by a small suspension bridge or, if permitted, by the unfinished concrete bridge. If the road below Zhangmu is in passable condition, a car from the Zhangmu Hotel takes its guests the 7 km. (4½ miles) to the bridge. A car from Kathmandu will be waiting on the other side if arrangements have been made well in advance, preferably through CITS in Lhasa. If the road below Zhangmu is impassable, as sometimes happens in the rainy season, travellers must walk down to the bridge. There are shortcuts between road levels, but it is a stiff downward climb. Porters to carry baggage can be hired easily in the town. The standard wage is 30 rupees per load as far as the Nepalese customs post on the other side of the river. The Zhangmu Hotel furnishes porters free of charge to guests under the care of CITS.

If no special car has been ordered from Kathmandu, travellers may have to walk or hitch-hike by truck to the Nepalese passport control post 4 km. (2½ miles) beyond the bridge at Kodari village, and the customs office several kilometres further at Tatopani. The road runs flat beside the river and it is not a difficult walk with porters to carry baggage.

A ride by truck can be arranged at Tatopani as far as Barahbise, an hour's drive south, where buses leave for Kathmandu four times a day. The last stage of the journey, by bus, takes about five hours. The time in Nepal is 1½ hours behind Tibet.

Tibet's Geography and Natural History

In geological terms the creation of the Himalayas and the rising of the Tibetan Plateau are extremely recent events. The mountains originated less than four million years ago, making them among the youngest in the world.

The abrupt and violent creation of mountains and plateau can be explained fairly simply. About 80 million years ago India broke away from an early massive proto-continent. Slowly and steadily it moved across the ancient Sea of Tethys, collecting hard sheets of rock on its way. Eventually, it rammed into the soft underside of Asia, which the rock easily penetrated and pushed up, creating the Himalayas. From sea level these rose rapidly to a height of nearly 9,000 m. (30,000 ft.). Today the succession of parallel ranges, running east to west for nearly 3,200 km (2,000 miles) reveals this original plate boundary between India and early Asia. In fact, the mass of sub-continental India is still forcing the Himalayas upwards at the remarkable rate of several inches a year.

The rivers of Tibet existed before the collision of India and Asia. As the soft sedimentary rocks which formed the bottom of the Sea of Tethys were folded up, the rivers were able to cut through them and maintain their original north-to-south course. (The Yarlong Tsangpo River is a major exception). As a result there are many spectacular gorges and mountain ranges that are sliced up into individual massifs.

Much of Tibet, once well-forested, lush and fertile, is today one of the world's most terrifying, unforgiving places. For as the Himalayas increased in height, less and less moisture reached the areas north of the range. The result has been a slow botanical death to the great northern plateau, the desertification of huge regions of Tibet and Xinjiang.

There are three clearly different geographical regions in Tibet (map, p.178), which as a whole far exceed the political borders.

By far the largest natural region is the Northern Plateau, or Chang Tang, an enormous expanse of over 1,000,000 sq. km. (386,100 sq.miles). It covers about half of Tibet's total surface area and is delineated in the west by the great Karakoram Range, in the north by the wall of the Astin Tagh, and in the northeast by the Nan Shan Range.

The Chang Tang undoubtedly has one of the worst climates on earth, with strong winds every day and bitterly cold temperatures throughout the year. There is little rainfall and no outlet for the rivers. As a result, it is characterised by myriad salty and brackish lakes.

These factors — constant wind, low rainfall and salt in the soil — severely limit the types of plant life that can survive: there are fewer than 60 species of flowering plants, only three of which are woody. Understandably, the flora is made up mostly of grasses and herbs.

Geographical Regions of Tibet

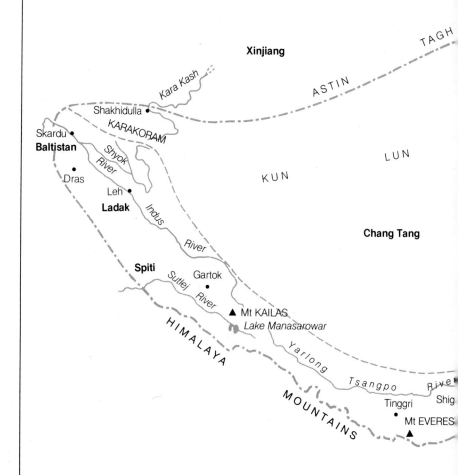

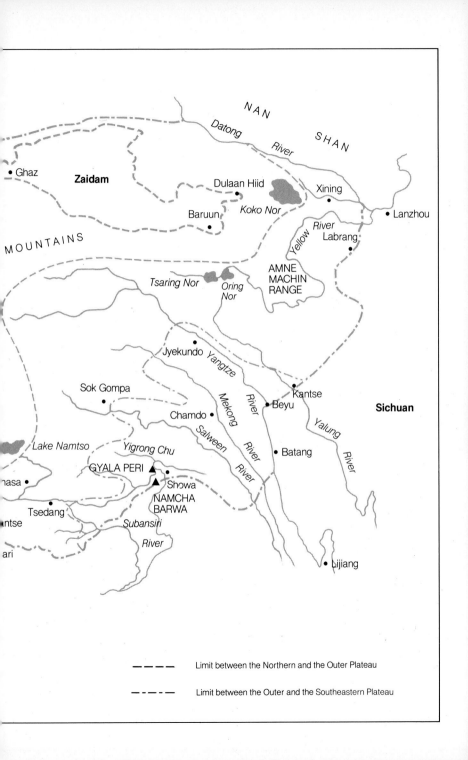

Limit between the Northern and the Outer Plateau

Limit between the Outer and the Southeastern Plateau

One outstanding feature of the Chang Tang is the Zaidam or "Salt Marsh" in the north. It used to be an enormous salt lake which has now mostly dried up, retaining some marshy areas. The Zaidam is distinguished by its large numbers of waterfowl and waders: more than 200 species of birds have been identified there.

It should be noted that most of the Chang Tang is never visited by humans. The hunters and nomads who live permanently on the Northern Plateau generally confine their wanderings to the southern and eastern parts of that great wilderness.

The second main geographical region of Tibet, the Outer Plateau, extends in a great arc for nearly 3,500 km (2,200 miles) from Baltistan in the west to beyond Xining, the capital of Qinghai, in the east. It is a relatively narrow strip, with the Himalayas forming the southern boundary. It is the most populous part of Tibet and contains almost all of the major human settlements.

The Outer Plateau differs from the Northern Plateau in several important ways. First, the temperature and climate are milder and consequently there is a richer floral and faunal distribution. Secondly, agriculture exists in the Outer Plateau and there are many old and well-developed agricultural regions. The area around Shigatse and the Lhasa Valley are clear examples of this. Contrary to popular images of Tibet, Lhasa has a pleasant climate with nearly all its rainfall coming in the summer. Most of the year it is entirely sunny and dry, mild during the day from April to October, and not unbearably cold in winter.

In the west, the Outer Plateau is an expanse of gravely land, where vegetation is poor, but in the east it becomes a grassy steppe, running all the way to the Yellow River, where there is more rainfall, warmer weather and significantly more vegetation.

The third and final geographical region is the Southeastern Plateau or "River Gorge Country". Although comprising only one-tenth of the total area of Tibet, plant and animal life here is vastly richer than in the other regions. Forests are very much a characteristic of the Southeastern Plateau; its western and northern boundaries follow the natural limits of trees.

The transition from the Outer Plateau to the Southeastern Plateau is gradual, though marked by a steady increase in trees and decline in altitude. The lowest point in Tibet — 1,615 m. (5,297 ft.) — lies near the great bend of the Yarlong Tsangpo River as it turns southward towards India. This region has an abundance of alpine and tropical plants such as laurels, rhododendrons, azaleas, bamboo, magnolias, oaks, and even tea and bananas, most of which appear in or near dense, moist, evergreen forests.

The most dramatic geographical phenomena here are the deep river gorges formed by the upper reaches of the Salween, Mekong and Yangzi, among Asia's mightiest rivers. These gorges erode and dissect the land, allowing moisture-bearing winds of the summer monsoon to reach the Southeastern Plateau.

Turning to the fauna of Tibet, many animal groups are impoverished because of the high altitude and severe climate. There is a very small number of amphibians and reptiles. Insects are few and so, therefore, are insectivorous birds (fly-catchers, swallows, swifts), moles and shrews. Fish are generally members of the salmon and carp family. They abound in rivers and some large lakes, such as Namtso (p.151) but in many lakes there is so much salt that no fish at all can survive.

Most of the species of wild animals in the Northern and Outer Plateau belong to desert and steppe fauna. These animals — particularly the hoofed variety — are well adapted to harsh conditions and the wide open landscapes that require them to migrate for long distances in search of food.

The shaggy, powerful yak is a shining example of animal adaptation to the awful demands of Tibet. Another typical animal is the *kiang*, or wild ass. It often gathers in large herds, especially in western Tibet, and makes extremely long journeys in search of pasture. The *kiang* is the fastest runner on the plateau. Another remarkable and very beautiful beast is the Tibetan antelope, outstanding for its long, thin, almost vertical horns that can attain 70 cm. (28 inches) in length.

The most numerous mammals in Tibet are rodents, which are ubiquitous wherever there is sufficient plant material to support them. Predators such as wolves, foxes and bears rely to a large extent on these rodents. Another predator, and perhaps the most magnificent of all Tibet's creatures, is the extremely rare snow leopard.

More than 500 species of birds have been recorded in Tibet and even the most casual observer can easily identify 20 or 30 separate varieties of birds. This number can quickly double with careful study or a visit to one of Tibet's great lakes.

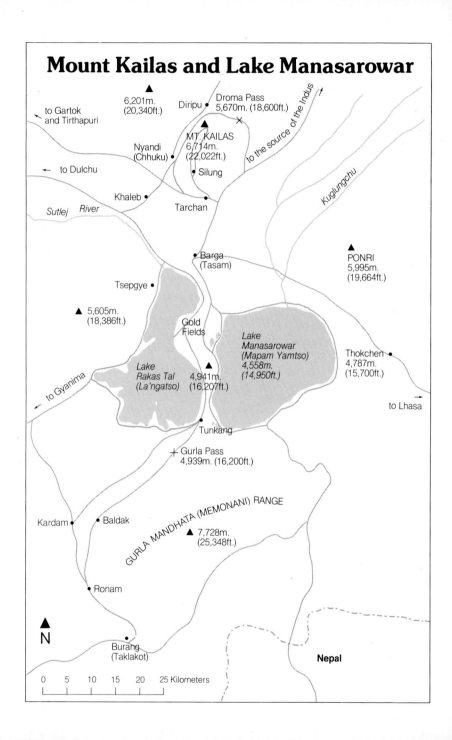

Mount Kailas and Lake Manasarowar

to Gartok
and Tirthapuri

6,201m.
(20,340ft.)

Diripu •

Droma Pass
5,670m. (18,600ft.)

to the source of the Indus

MT. KAILAS
6,714m.
(22,022ft.)

Nyandi
(Chhuku) •

• Silung

← to Dulchu

Kuglungchu

Khaleb •

Tarchan

Sutlej   River

• Barga
(Tasam)

PONRI
5,995m.
(19,664ft.)

Tsepgye •

▲ 5,605m.
(18,386ft.)

Gold
Fields

Lake
Manasarowar
(Mapam Yamtso)
4,558m.
(14,950ft.)

Thokchen •
4,787m.
(15,700ft.)

to Gyanima

Lake
Rakas Tal
(La'ngatso)

▲ 4,941m.
(16,207ft.)

to Lhasa

Tunkang

✛ Gurla Pass
4,939m. (16,200ft.)

GURLA MANDHATA (MEMONANI) RANGE

Kardam •

• Baldak

▲ 7,728m.
(25,348ft.)

• Ronam

▲
N

Burang
(Taklakot)

Nepal

0   5   10   15   20   25 Kilometers

Western Tibet

Just beyond the town of Lhatse the main road from Shigatse to Nepal divides. The left branch carries on in a southwesterly direction towards Tinggri and the border town of Zhangmu. The right branch is the all-important way to Western Tibet.

Few outsiders have travelled this route, but all of them have one destination in mind: Mount Kailas and Lake Manasarowar, 800 km. (500 miles) west of the Lhatse turn-off.

For thousands of years the Kailas area has been held sacred by Hindus, Buddhists and followers of Bon, Tibet's indigenous religion. Even today, pilgrims carry out devotional circumambulations here and converge on Mount Kailas by pilgrim paths from all over Tibet.

In their descriptions of this numinous mountain, Hindus consider it to be Siva's throne. Siva, one of three primary gods in Hinduism, sits in eternal paradise, the long strands of his matted hair falling and flowing all about him. The holy Ganges River is said to emanate from one of these strands.

Buddhist cosmography identifies Kailas with the mighty Mount Sumeru, central peak of the world. Holy Lake Manasarowar, the "mother-principle", represents Buddhist transcendent consciousness. The "father-mountain" itself represents the means to enlightenment.

As a Bon centre, Mount Kailas has enjoyed great popularity in the folk religion of Tibet. It is the soul of the country and assures perpetuity and protection for all the Tibetan people.

Physically, too, the area is outstanding. At 6,714 m. (22,022 ft.), Mount Kailas is one of the highest mountains in Western Tibet. Lake Manasarowar is generally recognised as the highest body of fresh water in the world. The Indus, Sutlej, Ganges and Yarlong Tsangpo (Brahmaputra) rivers, vital waterways for Tibet and South Asia, all originate on and around Mount Kailas.

The main local town is Burang (Taklakot), 110 km. (70 miles) south of Mount Kailas. There is a tourist office here and it will soon be possible to enter Nepal legally from this wild part of the central Himalayas.

Western Tibet as a whole is known as Ngari (Ali) District. Its administrative centre is at the town of Shiquanhe, 250 km. (155 miles) west of Mount Kailas on the road to Xinjiang.

Major Tibetan Festivals

Lunar Months

1st Month	1st- 7th	New Year Festival. Week-long drama and carnivals, horse races, archery.
1st Month	4th-25th	*Monlam* or Great Prayer Festival, begun by Tsong Khapa. Hordes of pilgrims at Lhasa's Jokhang.
1st Month	15th	Lantern Festival to commemorate Buddha's miracle at Sravasti. Fires on roofs, lamps in windows.
2nd Month	28th-29th	Festival to drive out evil and expel the scapegoat. Lamas encircle Lhasa with trumpets.
4th Month	7th	Important month for pilgrims. Birth of Buddha Sakyamuni.
4th Month	15th	Sakyamuni's enlightenment and entry to Nirvana. Outdoor opera. Captured animals set free.
5th Month	14th-16th	Hanging of giant *thangka* at Tashilhunpo, Shigatse.
5th Month	15th-24th	Worship of the Buddha. Bonfires and picnics under trees, at Norbulingka and parks.
6th Month	4th	Feast of Buddha's first sermon. Pilgrims climb holy mountains.
7th Month (end) and 8th Month		Golden Star Festival to wash away passion, greed, and jealousy. Ritual bathing in rivers. Picnics.
8th Month	1st-10th	*Dajyur* Festival at Gyantse and Damxung. Horse racing, games.
8th Month	1st- 7th	Harvest Festival. Prayers, dancing, singing, drinking.

9th Month	22nd	Buddha's descent from heaven after preaching to his mother. All monasteries open. Lots of pilgrims.
10th Month	25th	Memorial festival of Tsong Khapa's death. Fires on monastery roofs, many lamps.
12th Month	1st- 7th	New Year Festival at Shigatse.
12th Month	5th- 6th	Meeting of the Eight Guardians and demons. People stay indoors to avoid evil outside.
12th Month	29th	"Devil dance" day to drive out evil and the Old Year.

The Tibetan lunar calendar lags approximately four to six weeks behind the solar calendar. For example, Tibetan First Month usually falls in February, the Fifth Month in June or early July and the Eighth Month in September.

A Chronology of Events in Tibetan and Chinese History

TIBET

BC

500   Birth of Buddha in India

AD

173   Birth of Tho-tho-ri Nyantsen, 28th King of Tibet.

233   Tho-tho-ri Nyantsen receives a Buddhist scripture, marking
                   the initial introduction of Buddhism into Tibet, an event of
                   such importance that Tibetan currency notes were dated from
                   this year.

608-650   Reign of Songtsen Gampo, 32nd king. He sends scholars to
                   India to study Sanskrit and a Tibetan script is devised.

640   Tibet occupies Nepal.

641   Marriage of Songtsen Gampo to Chinese Princess, Wen
                   Cheng, daughter of Emperor Tai Zong. She and his
                   Nepalese wife influence the spread of Buddhism in Tibet.
                   Founding of the Jokhang.

645   Songtsen Gampo sends a minister to the Court of China
                   requesting permission to build a temple on Mt. Wu Tai in
                   Shansi Province. The request is granted.

654-676   Tibetan conquest of state of Tu-yu-lun and acquisition of
                   Chinese territories in Central Asia.

676-704   Tibetan expansion of Central Asian possessions and partial
                   reconquest of these by the Chinese.

704   Tride Tsugtsen (died 755) becomes king.

710   Tride Tsugtsen marries Chinese Princess, Chin-Cheng.

755-797   Reign of Trisong Detsen, Tride Tsugtsen's son. Reconquest
                   of Central Asian possessions.

763   Tibetans invade Chinese capital, Chang'an, and withdraw 15
                   days later.

779   Foundation of Monastery of Samye.
                   Buddhism recognised as state religion.

783   Peace treaty with China.

CHINA

BC

551   Birth of Confucius.

221   Qin Shi Huang Di becomes Emperor of all China.

AD

206-220   Western and Eastern Han Dynasties
The Three Kingdoms — spread of influence of Buddhism.

265-419   Jin Dynasties.

420-589   Northern and Southern Dynasties.

589-618   Sui Dynasty

618-906   Tang Dynasty

627-649   Emperor Tai Zong
629 Xuanzhuang (Hsuan-tsang), pilgrim-traveller-translator, one of the great figures in the history of Chinese Buddhism, leaves China for India, returning in 645.
634 Tibetans send envoys and tribute to China.
635 A-lo-pen, Nestorian monk, arrives at Tang Court.
641 Marriage of Tai Zong's daughter, Princess Wen Cheng, to Songtsen Gampo of Tibet, followed by 20 years of peace between China and Tibet.

650-683   Emperor Gao Zong. During his reign Taoism given precedence over Buddhism; China's prestige continues at its zenith. The first Jews and Arabian Muslims make their appearance in China.
670 A major campaign in Gansu against Tibetans ends in disaster.
679 Tibetans driven from Tarim Kingdoms.

684-701   Empress Wu attempts to make Buddhism the state religion. Extensive translations of Buddhist texts made.

707-710   Peace settlement with Tibetans, and Princess Chin-Cheng's marriage to Tride Tsugtsen.

785-805	Tibetan army advances westward to the Pamirs as far as the Oxus River.
797	Muni Tsangpo, Trisong Detsen's son, becomes king.
799-815	Reign of Sadneleg.
815-836	Reign of Ralpachen, son of Sadneleg. Intense activity of translation of Buddhist texts.
821	Peace treaty with China; the Tibetans retain most of their Central Asian possessions.
836-842	Reign of Lang Darma, brother of Ralpachen. As a supporter of the Bon religion, he severely persecutes Buddhism.
842-1247	Lang Darma murdered. Struggle for power ensues with small factions constantly warring or allying with each other.
978	Rinchen Tsangpo, a famous translator, invites Indian teachers to western Tibet, marking the beginning of the renaissance of Buddhism. Monasteries are established in western Tibet.
1040	Birth of Milarepa (died 1123), great Tibetan poet and mystic.
1042	Atisha (died 1054), a great Mahayana teacher from India, arrives in Tibet and carries out missionary activities in western and central Tibet.
1057	Establishment of Reting Monastery.
1071	Founding of Sakya Monastery.
1182	Birth of Sakya Pandit (died 1251), learned scholar of the Sakya sect.
1207	Tibetans send delegation to Genghis Khan. Friendly relations and tribute are established.
1227	Death of Genghis Khan. Tibetans cease paying tribute to Mongols.
1244	Sakya Pandit invited to meet Mongol Khan, and invested with temporal power over central Tibet.
1252-1253	Mongol invasion.
1254	Kublai Khan grants Phagspa Lodro Gyaltsen (1235-1280), Sakya Pandit's nephew, supreme authority over Tibet, thus forming a politico-religious relationship between the Mongols and the Tibetans (which later developed into the patron-lama link between the Manchu emperors and the Dalai Lama).

712-756	Emperor Xuan Zong Tibetans attack Lanzhou and are defeated. Xuan Zong distrusts Tibetans and resists future peace settlements for many years. 730 Treaty negotiated with Tibetans.
756-763	An Lu Shan Rebellion — abdication of Xuan Zong.
763	Tibetans invade and occupy the capital Chang'an and then withdraw.
783	Peace treaty with Tibet.
860-874	Uprisings in China.
907-960	Five Dynasties 955 Great persecution of Buddhists.
960-1280	Sung Dynasty — development of Neo-Confucianism.
1189	Genghis Khan (1167-1227) becomes leader of the Mongols.
1271-1294	Marco Polo in China.
1280-1368	Yuan Dynasty: Kublai Khan becomes Emperor of China. 1295 Kublai Khan dies.

1354	Fighting breaks out between the Sakyapa sect and the powerful Lang family. The might of the Sakyapa sect declines and a re-organisation of the state takes place.
1357	Birth of Tsong Khapa (died 1419), founder of the Gelugpa or Yellow Hat sect.
1391	Birth of Gedun Truppa (died 1474), disciple of Tsong Khapa and head of the Gelugpa sect. Posthumously named as the first Dalai Lama.
1409	Founding of Ganden Monastery.
1416	Founding of Drepung Monastery.
1419	Founding of Sera Monastery.
1434-1534	Constant power struggles, lasting more than 100 years, between the provinces of U and Tsang, whose leaders adhered to the Gelugpa and Karmapa sects respectively.
1447	Founding of Tashilhunpo Monastery.
1475	Birth of Second Dalai Lama, Gedun Gyatso (died 1542).
1543	Birth of Third Dalai Lama, Sonam Gyatso (died 1588). He visits Mongolia where Altan Khan confers the title "Dalai Lama" on him.
1582	Founding of Kumbum Monastery.
1588	Birth of Fourth Dalai Lama, Yonten Gyatso (died 1616), conveniently the great-grandson of Altan Khan and the only non-Tibetan in the line of Dalai Lamas.
1617	Birth of Fifth Dalai Lama, Ngawang Lozang Gyatso (died 1682), builder of the Potala. Collapse of the province of U and victory to the Tsang provincial forces resulting in a growth of power of the Karmapa sect.
1624-1636	Jesuit missionaries arrive in western Tibet. 1641-1642 Gusri Khan of the Qosot Mongols overthrows King of Tsang and hands territory over to Dalai Lama.
1642-1659	Consolidation of the Tibetan theocracy. Many Karmapa sect monasteries handed over to the Gelugpa sect. Abbot of Tashilhunpo Monastery given title of Panchen Lama by the Dalai Lama.
1652	Fifth Dalai Lama visits China.

1368-1644	Ming Dynasty
1403-1424	Emperor Yong Le moves capital to Peking.
1519	First Portuguese presented to Emperor Wu Zong.
1601	Jesuit Matteo Ricci gains access to the Chinese Court.
1644-1911	Qing Dynasty
1644-1662	Emperor Shun Zhi
1663-1722	Emperor Kang Xi
1670-1750	Chinese conquest of Mongolia and Xinjiang and occupation of Lhasa.

1682	Death of Fifth Dalai Lama; his death is kept secret by the Regent.
1683	Birth of Sixth Dalai Lama, Tsangyang Gyatso.
1697	The Sixth Dalai Lama enthroned after death of Fifth Dalai Lama made public.
1705	The Khan of Qosot, Lhajang Khan, invades Tibet and conquers Lhasa.
1706	The Khan of Qosot deposes Sixth Dalai Lama and sends him to China, but he dies on the way. The Khan declares Sixth Dalai Lama not to have been a true reincarnation and enthrones a monk of his own choice.
1707	Italian Capuchin monks arrive in Tibet.
1708	Another reincarnation of Sixth Dalai Lama discovered. For reasons of security he takes refuge in Kumbum Monastery.
1716	Jesuit Father Ippolito Desideri arrives in Lhasa.
1717-1720	Dzungar Mongols occupy and sack Lhasa, killing the Khan of Qosot. The Manchu Emperor of China deposes the Dalai Lama appointed by the Khan of Qosot and recognises claimant from Kumbum Monastery (Kelzang Gyatso), who is officially recognised as Seventh Dalai Lama in 1720.
1733-1747	Pholhanas (died 1747) brings internal struggles to an end and with the support of the Chinese, becomes effective ruler of Tibet.
1751	After an attempted revolt against the Chinese garrison, Dalai Lama is recognised as ruler of Tibet but without effective political power.
1757	Seventh Dalai Lama dies.
1758	Birth of Eighth Dalai Lama, Jompal Gyatso (died 1804).
1774-1775	First British Mission to Tibet led by George Bogle.
1783-1784	British Mission led by Samuel Turner. Chinese troops impose the Peace of Kathmandu following Gurkha incursions into Tibet.
1806-1815	The Ninth Dalai Lama, Lungtok Gyatso.
1811-1812	Thomas Manning, British explorer, reaches Lhasa.
1816-1837	The 10th Dalai Lama, Tsultrim Gyatso.

1723   Christianity proscribed in China.

1793   Lord MacCartney leads a British mission to China.

1795   White Lotus Rebellion.

1834   Lord Napier's mission skirmishes with the Chinese.

1835   Birth of Empress Ci Xi (died 1908).

1839   Opium War between China and Britain begins.

1842   Treaty of Nanking concluded between China and Britain.

1843   Hong Kong ceded to Britain.

1850-1864   Taiping Rebellion.

1857   British and French troops occupy Canton.

1838-1856	The 11th Dalai Lama, Khedrup Gyatso.
1846	Lazarist monks, Huc and Gabet, arrive in Lhasa.
1854-1856	Conflict with Nepal.
1856-1875	The 12th Dalai Lama, Trinley Gyatso.
1876	Birth of 13th Dalai Lama, Thupten Gyatso (died 1933). Diplomatic conflict between Russia and Britain over contacts and privileges with Tibet.
1890	British Protectorate over Sikkim.
1904	British military expedition, under Col. Younghusband, forces its way to Lhasa. Dalai Lama flees to Mongolia. Conclusion of agreement with Abbot of Ganden Monastery.
1909	Dalai Lama returns to Lhasa.
1910	Restoration of Chinese control over eastern Tibet and dispatch of troops to Lhasa.
1911	Tibetan uprising against Chinese.
1912	Dalai Lama returns to Lhasa, ruling without Chinese influence.
1913-1914	Conference of Simla with British, Chinese and Tibetan plenipotentiaries: Chinese refuse to ratify agreement.
1920-1921	Mission of Sir Charles Bell to Tibet.
1923	Panchen Lama flees to China.
1933	Death of 13th Dalai Lama.
1934	Appointment of Regent (Abbot of Reting Monastery).
1935	Birth of 14th Dalai Lama, Tenzin Gyatso — enthroned in 1940.
1947	Indian independence and end of the British Tibet Policy.
1950	Dalai Lama flees to border with Sikkim. Returns to Lhasa after receiving assurances from Chinese Government.
1951	Arrival of People's Liberation Army in Lhasa.
1954	Dalai Lama visits Peking.
1959	Attempted uprising. Dalai Lama flees to India.
1964	Tibet becomes an "autonomous region" of the People's Republic of China Dalai Lama remains in exile.

1858	Treaties signed with Britain, France, Russia and the United States, extending special foreign privileges.
1860	British and French troops occupy Peking.
1862	Beginning of Tong Zhi Restoration and Self-strengthening Movement.
1893	Birth of Mao Zedong.
1894-1895	Sino-Japanese War — China defeated.
1898	Abortive "Hundred Days" ends short period of liberal reform.
1899-1900	Boxer Rebellion.
1905	Sun Yat-sen (1866-1925) organises anti-Manchu revolutionary movement in Japan.
1911	Manchu Dynasty overthrown. Chinese Republic founded.
1915	Yuan Shikai (died 1916), President of China, proclaims himself Emperor.
1917	China declares war on Germany.
1921	Kuomintang revived. Chinese Communist Party founded.
1931	Japanese occupy Manchuria.
1934	Red Army's "Long March" begins.
1937	Sino-Japanese War begins.
1945	Civil War between Communists and Kuomintang resumes.
1949	Founding of The People's Republic of China.
1966-1976	Cultural Revolution.
1976	Death of Chairman Mao Zedong.

Tibetan Glossary

by Milan M. Melvin

The following list of Tibetan words and phrases is all too brief but sufficient for you to acquire the basic necessities and, depending on your inclination, to get out of or into trouble. Tibetans are wonderful, fun-loving people and even this small snatch of their language can launch you into some unforgettable relationships.

Pronunciation

The vowel "a" must be pronounced like the "a" in "father" — soft and long, unless it appears as -ay, in which case it is pronounced as in "say "or "day". A slash through a letter indicates the neutral vowel sound uh.

Word Order

Simple Tibetan sentences are constructed as follows:

Noun (or pronoun)	Object	Verb
I	mountains	going
Nga	kang ree la	dro ge ray

The verb is always last.

Verb Tenses

Tibetan verbs are composed of two parts: the root, which carries the meaning of the verb, and the ending, which indicates the tense (past, present, or future). The simplest and most common verb form, consisting of the root plus the ending -ge ray, can be used for the present and future tenses. The root is strongly accented in speech. In order to form the past tense, substitute the ending -song.

"nyo ge ray" means, loosely, "buying, going to buy"

"nyo song " means "bought"

Only the verb roots are given in this glossary; remember to add the appropriate endings.

Pronouns

I Nga
you (singular) kirang
he, she, it korang, ko

we nga-tso
you (plural) kirang-tso
they korong-tso
this dee la

my, mine nge, ngay, narang kee
your, yours (singular) kirang kee
his, hers, its korang kee
our, ours narang-tso yee
your, yours (plural) kirang-tso yee
their, theirs korong-tso yee

Relations

name   ming la
child   poo goo
boy   poo
girl   po mo
man, husband   cho ga
woman, wife   kyee men
brother   poon dya
sister   poon kya, ah jee la
father   pa ba, pa la
mother   ah ma

Time

minute   ka ma
hour   tchø zø
day   nyee ma, shak ma
week   døn ta
month   da wa
year   lo
day before yesterday   ke nyee ma
yesterday   ke sang
last night   dang gong
today   ta ring
tomorrow   sang nyee, sang
day after tomorrow   nang nyee
now   tanda, ta ta
always   tak par
morning   sho kay
afternoon   nyeen goon

Numbers

one   cheek
two   nee
three   soom
four   shee
five   nga
six   trook
seven   døn
eight   gye, kay
nine   koo,goo
ten   tchoo
eleven   tchoop cheek
twelve   tchoog nee
thirteen   tchook soom
fourteen   tchoop shee
fifteen   tchoo nga
sixteen   tchoo trook
seventeen   tchoop don
eighteen   tchup kyay
nineteen   tchur koo
twenty   nee shoo tamba
twenty-one   nee shoo sak cheek
twenty-two   nee shoo sak nee
twenty-three   nee shoo sak soom
twenty-four   nee shoo sup shee
twenty-five   nee shoo say nga
twenty-six   nee shoo sar trook
twenty-seven   nee shoo sub døn
twenty-eight   nee shoo sap kay
twenty-nine   nee sar koo
thirty   soom tchoo tamba
forty   sheep joo tamba
fifty   ngup tchoo tamba
sixty   trook tchoo tamba
seventy   døn tchoo tamba
eighty   kyah joo tamba
ninety   koop tchoo tamba
one hundred   gyah tamba
two hundred   nee gyah
three hundred   soom gyah

Food

barley   droo, nay
roasted barley flour   tsampa
beef   lang sha
breakfast   sho kay ka lak
butter   mar
cheese   choo ra
chicken meat   cha sha
chili peppers   mar tsa
cigarette   ta mak
corn   droo
egg   go nga
flour   to sheep, pak pay
food   ka lak
fruit   shing dong
lunch   nyeen goong ka lak
dinner   kong dak ka lak
meat   sha
milk   o ma
millet   ko do
onion   tsong
potato   sho ko

rice   dray
sugar   chee ma ka ra
tea   cha
vegetables   ngup tsay, tsay
wheat   tro, dro
delicious   shimbo

Other Nouns

bag   gye mo, gye wa
blanket   nya tee, gam lo, nye zen
book (common)   teb
book (religious)   pay zya
boots   som ba, lam
bridge   sam ba
cave   trak poo, poo goo
dog   kee, kyee
donkey   poon goo
fire   may
house   kang ba
hill   ree
kerosene   sa noom
kettle   tib lee
knife   tee, tree
lake   tso
matches   moo see, tsak ta
medicine   men
   pill   ree poo
moon   da wa
mountain   kang ree
mountain pass   la
cooking pot   hai yoom, rak sang
rain   char pa
river   tsang po, tchoo, chu
rock   do
room   kang mee
snow   kang, ka
spoon   tur ma, too ma
star   kar ma
stomach   tro ko
sun   nyee ma
thread   koo ba
Tibet   Pø la
Tibetan people   Pø pa
Tibetan language   Pø kay
trail   lam ga
umbrella   nyee doo
water   tchoo, chu

Westerner   in gee, pee ling
wind   loong bo chem bo
wood   shing
candle   yang la
cup   mok, cha gar

Verbs

arrive   lep
bring   kay sho
buy   nyo
carry   kay
feel cold   cha
come   yong
cook   ka lak so
drink   toong
eat   shay sa
forget   jay, chay
get up   lang
give   tay, nang
be hungry   tro ko tok
learn   lap
look   meek tang
make, fix   so
see   ton
sell   tsong
be sick   na
sit, stay   day, shook
teach   lap
go   dro, do
wait   goo
work   le ka chee

Adjectives

lost   lak song
thirsty   ka kam
good   yak po
bad   yak po min doo
big   chem bo
small   choon choon
weak   shook choon choon
strong   shyook chem bo
empty   tong ba
full   kang
beautiful   dzay bo
expensive   gong chem bo
cold   trang mo
hot   tsa bo

different   kye per, cheek be ma ray
same   nang shing
few   tet see tet see
much, many   mang bo
light   yang bo, yang
heavy   jee po, jee ba tsa po

Adverbs
up   ya la
down   ma la
near   nye bo
far   ta ring bo, gyang bo
here   deh roo
there   pa roo, pa ge
left   yom ba
right   yay ba
slow   ka lee
quickly   dyok po, dyok po
really, very   she ta, she tai

Miscellaneous
and   tang, ta
another   yang ya
how much, how many   ka tzø
maybe   cheek chay na
sometimes   tsam tsam
other   shem ba, shen da, yem ba
what   ka ray
where from   ka ne
where to   ka ba, ka par, ka roo
who   soo
why   ka ray chay nay

Phrases
hello!,   greetings!   tashi delay
enough!,   stop!   deek song
finished   tsar song, deek song
I do not understand   ha ko ma song
I understand, I know   ha ko gee doo,
   ha ko song
right!, really!, yes   ray, la ray
very important   kay chembo, ne ka
   chem bo
what is this called?   dee ming
la ka ray see ge ray? dee ka ra ray?
how much is (this)?   (dee la) gong ka
   tzø ray?

it doesn't matter   kay kay chee ge
   ma ray, kay kay so ge ma ray
be careful, slowly   ka lee ka lee
I am hungry   nge tro ko to kee doo
are/is there any (onions)   (tsong)
   doo-ay, (tsong) doog-ay?
please bring (onions)   (tsong)
   kay sho ah
o.k., thanks   la so
goodnight   sim jam, sim jam nang
   ro
how far is (Lhasa)?   (Lhasa la)
   gyan lø yø ray?
how are you?   kirang sook po day bo
   yeen bay?, kirang ko sook day be
   yeen bay?
I am fine   sook po day bo yeen, day
   bo doo

Recommended Reading

General History, Religion and Culture

Bell, Charles. *The People of Tibet* (Oxford: Oxford University Press, 1928).

Bell, Charles. *The Religion of Tibet* (Oxford: Oxford University Press, 1931).

David-Neel, Alexandra. *Magic and Mystery in Tibet* (New York: Dover, 1971).

Snellgrove, David and Richardson, Hugh. *A Cultural History of Tibet* (Boulder: Prajna Press, 1980).

Stein, R.A. *Tibetan Civilization* (Stanford University Press, 1972).

Tucci, Giuseppe. *The Religions of Tibet* (London: Routledge & Kegan Paul, 1980).

Waddell, L. Austine. *Buddhism and Lamaism of Tibet* (Kathmandu: Educational Enterprise (Pvt) Ltd., 1985).

Religion

Conze, Edward. *A Short History of Buddhism* (London: George Allen & Unwin Ltd., 1982).

David-Neel, Alexandra. *Initiations and Initiates in Tibet* (Berkeley: Shambhala Publications, 1970).

Evans-Wentz, W.Y. *The Tibetan Book of the Dead* (London: Oxford University Press, 1957).

Evans-Wentz, W.Y. *Tibet's Great Yogi Milarepa* (London: Oxford University Press, 1969).

Tucci, Giuseppe. *The Theory and Practice of the Mandala* (New York: Sam Weiser, Inc., 1970).

Art

Gordon, Antoinette K. *The Iconography of Tibetan Lamaism* (Tokyo and Rutland: C.E. Tuttle Co., 1959).

Pal, Pratapaditya. *Art of Tibet* (Los Angeles: L.A. County Museum of Art, 1983).

Tarthang Tulku. *Sacred Art of Tibet* (Berkeley: Dharma Publishing, 1974).

Tucci, Giuseppe. *Transhimalaya* (Geneva: Nagel Publishers, 1973).

Natural History and Exploration

Cameron, Ian. *Mountains of the Gods* (London: Century, 1984).

Miller, Luree. *On Top of the World, Five Women Explorers of Tibet* (London: Paddington Press, 1976).

Schaller, George. *Stones of Silence* (New York: Viking, 1980).

Vaurie, Charles. *Tibet and Its Birds* (London: H.F. & G. Witherby Ltd., 1972).

Travel

Allen, Charles. *A Mountain in Tibet* (London: Futura, 1983).

Byron, Robert. *First Russia, Then Tibet* (New York: Penguin, 1985).

Harrer, Heinrich. *Seven Years in Tibet* (New York: E.P. Dutton, 1954).

Hopkirk, Peter. *Trespassers on the Roof of the World* (Oxford: Oxford University Press, 1982).

Tibet since 1950

Avedon, John F. *In Exile From the Land of Snows* (London: Michael Joseph, 1984).

Dalai Lama. *My Land and My People* (New York: Potala Corp., 1983).

Photography

Bonavia, David and Bartlett, Magnus. *Tibet* (London: Thames and Hudson Ltd., 1981).

Dalai Lama. *Tibet: the Sacred Realm* (New York: Aperture, 1983).

Kling, Kevin. *Tibet* (London: Thames and Hudson Ltd., 1985)

Tung, Rosemary Jones. *A Portrait of Lost Tibet* (London: Thames and Hudson Ltd., 1980).

Health

Hackett, Peter H. *Mountain Sickness — Prevention, Recognition and Treatment* (New York: The American Alpine Club, 1980).

Useful Addresses

Lhasa

Travel Permits and Visas

Public Security Bureau
Zhongxue Lu, tel.23170
公安局外事科　中学路

Foreign Affairs Bureau
Jianshe Lu, tel.24992
西藏外办　建设路

Nepalese Consulate
13 Norbulingka Lu, tel.22880
尼泊尔领事馆
罗布林卡路13号

Transport

CAAC
88 Jiefang Lu, tel.22417
中国民航局　解放路88号

CITS
Number 3 Guesthouse,
tel.22980/24406
中国国际旅行社　区三所

Lhasa Travel Service Company
Yanhe Dong Lu, tel.23632
拉萨市旅游公司　沿河东路

"Taxi Company"
Xingfu Dong Lu, tel.23762
拉萨市出租汽车公司
幸福东路

Bus Station
Jiefang Lu, tel. 22756/22757
拉萨客运站　解放路

Banks

Bank of China
17 Yanhe Dong Lu, tel.22263
中国银行　沿河东路17号

Lhasa Hotel Bank
Lhasa Hotel, Minzu Lu,
tel.2221
拉萨饭店　民族路

Post and Telecommunications

Central Post Office
(You Dian Da Lou)
Linkuo Lu, tel.113
邮电大楼长途台　林廓路

Post Office
100 Xingfu Dong Lu,
tel.23293
邮电局营业科
幸福东路100号

Hospitals

Regional Military Hospital
Jiefang Bei Lu
at Sera Monastery
军区总医院　解放北路
（色拉寺）

People's Hospital
10 Jianshe Lu,
tel.22353/23353
区人民医院　建设路10号

Shops and Services

General Department Store
Jiefang Lu, tel.23380
拉萨市百货商场　解放路

Nong Ken Ting Department
Store
Renmin Lu
农垦厅商店　人民路

Bookstore, Renmin Lu
新华书店　人民路

"Selling Department for
Tourist Products"
Xingfu Dong Lu
销售部旅游产品　幸福东路

Tent and Banner Factory
just off Xingfu Dong Lu
城关区儿童服装衣厂

Public Showers
Renmin Lu (across from
No. 1 Guesthouse)
公共浴室　人民路

Laundry Service
Renmin Lu
(behind public showers)
拉萨市服务公司洗染厂

Chengdu

CITS
180 Renmin Nan Lu
tel.29653/25914,
tlx.60154 CITCD CN
中国国际旅行社
人民南路180号

CAAC
31 Bei Xin Jie, tel.3087/3038
中国民航局　北新街31号

Railway, North Station
Renmin Bei Lu, tel.92633
火车站（北站）　人民北路

Jinjiang Hotel
180 Renmin Nan Lu, tel.24481
锦江饭店　人民南路180号

Index